Praying Grace

training for personal ministry

Praying Grace

training for personal ministry

terry teykl

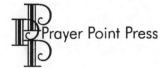
Prayer Point Press

Praying Grace
Training for Personal Ministry
Copyright © 2002 Dr. Terry Teykl
Published by Prayer Point Press

First Printing, May 2002
Second Printing, September 2003
Third Printing, August 2004
Fourth Printing, September 2005
Fifth Printing, February 2008

Unless otherwise indicated, all scripture quotations are from the Holy Bible, New International Version © 1973, 1978, 1984 by the International Bible Society. Used by permission of Zondervan Publishing House.

ISBN: 1-57892-110-4
Printed in the United States of America

Prayer Point Press
2100 N. Carrolton Dr.
Muncie, IN 47304
Phone: (765) 759-0215
To order, call toll free: (888) 656-6067
or visit www.prayerpointpress.com

To Gary and Sally Herman
who "wrote the book" on praying grace
long before I wrote the book.

LET US THEN APPROACH THE THRONE OF GRACE WITH CONFIDENCE,
SO THAT WE MAY RECEIVE MERCY AND FIND GRACE
TO HELP US IN OUR TIME OF NEED.
—HEBREWS 4:16

CONTENTS

UNIT ONE - FOUNDATIONS

FOUNDATIONS - PRAYER AS A MINISTRY

1

I have always believed that when Jesus cleared the money changers out of the temple in his most remembered show of "righteous anger," he was more concerned about the absence of ministry in the Lord's house than the presence of money. Not that he was necessarily happy about the temple serving as the Jerusalem stock exchange, but that practice had been going on for years. Jesus' indignation stemmed from something deeper than the obvious.

Jesus encountered needy people constantly, in the streets, in the marketplace, in their homes, and probably at the temple. He may have stepped over them as he climbed the stairs to the entrance. The sick, the lonely, the oppressed—where else would they go hoping to receive a touch from God? But in the "house of God," did they find him? Did anyone reach out a hand or offer a prayer? Did anyone listen with empathy? Did anyone even notice them?

Full of compassion and frustration, Jesus exhorted "My house will be called a house of *prayer*..." (Matthew 21:13, italics mine), and then to emphasize the point, he healed the blind and the lame who came to him (Matthew 21:14). He wanted people to be ministered to and prayed for. He wanted his house to be a place where one could discover and experience the love of the Father. The religious leaders were concerned about all the wrong things, yet they were too arrogant and full of pride to receive correction. A tactful note in the suggestion box would have had little or no effect at all. Jesus' fiery display that day may not have changed their ways much, but they could not have easily forgotten his words.

Unfortunately, this same scene might replay itself over and over if Jesus were to visit many churches today. Though our problem may not be money changers and tax collectors, I must question whether we are doing any better at addressing the needs of people than they were in Matthew 21.

Every Sunday our churches are filled with people who are run over by life. They wear a smile on

JESUS WANTS HIS HOUSE (THE CHURCH) TO BE A HOUSE OF _____.

QUESTION

WHY WAS JESUS ANGRY AT THE TEMPLE?

their face to hide the hurt of marital problems, abusive relationships, children who have turned away, financial failures and terminal illnesses. Week after week, they come to church desperately needing a touch from God, and often leave in the same condition in which they arrived. How tragic it is when broken humanity passes through our doors only to receive a bulletin and a nice, three point sermon!

I first wrote that paragraph in a book called *Blueprint for the House of Prayer* five years ago. And even though some churches are ministering to the needs of people effectively, many still can't grasp the concept of personal ministry. People come; people go. They carry their problems in and they carry them back out. They may hear the truth, but they are not afforded the chance to apply it to their wounds. They hear *about* God and what he *can* do, but they are never invited to experience him personally.

> *They hear* about *God and what he* can *do, but they are never invited to experience him personally.*

For example, I preached in a church in Texas recently on how the righteousness of Jesus covers our shame. Toward the end of my sermon, I began to notice tears and sniffles all around the room. Something I was saying was hitting home and people were responding to the pain that was surfacing in their spirits. And I was excited because I knew God wanted to heal that pain for many of those people. That's just how he is—he loves us and doesn't want us carrying around toxic baggage.

But as I concluded, instead of moving with the Spirit into a very natural time of ministry, the pastor met me on the platform with a big smile, asked if anyone wanted to join the church, and quickly launched into the benediction. It was 12:00 noon—church was over.

I wondered if he ever really looked at their faces, that day or any day. I tried not to let mine reflect my thoughts. I wanted to

 NOTES

throw his hymnal out the window and say, *"What is wrong with you? Don't you see these people need prayer? Isn't that what we sing for, preach for and come here for, so that God can touch lives in a meaningful way?"* But as a guest in his pulpit, there was nothing I could do. Off to Luby's we went.

In a different church where I was somewhat reluctantly allowed to do some personal ministry in the choir room after I preached, I had another disheartening experience. An elderly man came to me for prayer, explaining that his wife of fifty years had left him several weeks before and he was hurt, angry and lonely. His family was far away and he had few close friends he could talk to. So we prayed together and he wept. I could almost sense his relief as I listened to his story and prayed over him. When I finished, the man wrapped his arms around me and held on, sobbing. "Thank you," he choked. "I've been in church every Sunday since she left, but no one has offered to pray for me. I really needed that."

Jesus still wants his house to be a house of prayer. He still wants to touch people the way he did the leper (Mark 1:41) and the children (Mark 10:16). He wants to heal and bless, and he wants people to experience the redeeming, reassuring grace of the Father. But he needs us to be his hands. He needs carpenters, business people, nurses, accountants, secretaries, store clerks, executives and doctors. He needs all who are willing to be yielded and available to reach out to someone and say, "Can I pray for you?"

THE BIRTH OF PERSONAL MINISTRY

From the very beginning of the church, personal prayer ministry was meant to be a cornerstone of the gospel message. How do we know? In order to put it into proper perspective, we must look at the sequence of events following Jesus' resurrection as recorded in the first several chapters of Acts.

In Acts 1, Jesus ascends into heaven after giving final instructions to his disciples. The disciples return to Jerusalem to wait,

PRAYER IS A MEANS OF GRACE.
—JOHN WESLEY

pray, and prepare for what lies ahead. In Acts chapter 2, the Holy Spirit is poured out at Pentecost, and the disciples emerge from the Upper Room supernaturally empowered to spread the gospel. The church is born as Peter preaches to a large crowd and many thousand believe his message and are saved.

In the next passage in Acts 3, Peter and John are going to the temple to pray at 3:00 in the afternoon, when they encounter a lame beggar at one of the city gates. But it was not just any city gate—it was the gate called Beautiful, an ornate, bronze-sheathed archway of vines and fruit that was one of the more popular entrances to the city.

Peter and John both noticed the man, and then Peter said to him, "Look at us! Silver or gold I do not have, but what I have I give you. In the name of Jesus Christ of Nazareth, walk" (Acts 3:4, 6). Then the beggar got up and began "walking and jumping, and praising God" (Acts 3:8). As he ran into the city to buy his first pair of sandals, many people saw him and recognized him as the man who was lame, and in their amazement, hurried to hear what Peter and John had to say. After hearing about Jesus, they too were saved.

This story is significant for several reasons. First, it marks the beginning of personal ministry as carried out by Jesus' followers after his departure from earth. He said, "I tell you the truth, anyone who has faith in me will do what I have been doing. He will do even greater things than these..." (John 14:12). And no sooner had he left than he made good on his promise in a visible way through the hands of Peter and John.

Second, this story holds a prominent place in the birth and formation of the church as we know it. Its front page billing in Acts— right after Pentecost—indicates the importance of the event. It was not only proof of the validity of Jesus' promise in John, it was an example for us to follow. The disciples were empowered by the Holy Spirit in large part to carry on Jesus' ministry of compassion and prayer. He bestowed on them his own abilities, in-

ILLUSTRATION

Dr. Margaret Poloma, a sociologist from the University of Akron, surveyed 909 people from over twenty countries who attended services at the Toronto Airport Christian Fellowship church. Here's what she found:

90% stated they had experienced changes in their lives which they could attribute to their visit (they described increases in spiritual refreshment, holiness, healing, evangelism and social outreach)

91% said they had a greater sense of the Father's love

89% testified to being more in love with Jesus than ever before

1% received salvation

28% reported recommitting their lives to Christ

22% claimed to have received some type of healing

 NOTES

spired by the Holy Spirit, so that they could minister to the needs of people just as he had done. He intended for his church to pray for the needy to demonstrate by their deeds the gospel they were preaching.

Finally, the account of the healing that took place at the gate Beautiful fulfilled Jesus' words, "I am the vine; you are the branches. If a man remains in me and I in him, he will bear much fruit; apart from me you can do nothing. This is to my Father's glory, that you bear much fruit, showing yourselves to be my disciples" (John 15:5, 8).

It is no coincidence that this miracle took place at the foot of the bronze trellis of branches and vines. It was truly a beautiful structure, no doubt brilliant in the afternoon sun. It stood as a symbol of God's words to Israel in the Old Testament (Isaiah 5:2-7). He expected Israel to bear fruit like a healthy vine and thereby glorify him in the earth. However, up to that point, the idea was, like the gate, purely ornamental.

> *It is by grace that we can pray, and by grace that others can receive through our prayers.*

But when Peter and John stood beneath that spectacular vine and reached out to the lame beggar in compassion, they became the branches—extensions of Jesus—bearing good fruit in his name. They gave new life, not just to the man who could now walk, but to the symbol of Jesus' continued work in the earth.

Jesus did not come to let us taste the wonders of heaven, only to lock them away forever when he left. No! He came that we might have abundant life right now. He prayed to the Father, "Your kingdom come and be established on this earth just like it is in heaven." And then he showed us that our job in the process is to pray, inviting God to move and work in our lives and the lives of those around us. We are called to be branches of this same Jesus, bearing good fruit in his name.

PRAYER WEARS DENIM

I love the way David Jeremiah characterizes prayer:

> Jesus is teaching us that prayer is not just for church on Sunday. It is not offered only before some shrine. Prayer wears denim work clothes. It is about day-to-day living. The issues we pray about stem from needs in our daily experience. Prayer is about everyday things, about bread and about money.

> Prayer is about real-world concerns, spoken in real-world language. God does not want us to shift into a stained-glass prayer voice to address Him. Prayer comes out of this world, the workaday world of houses and cars and grass and sewer lines and schools and janitors and the IRS.

In Acts 3, Peter and John put on their workclothes and demonstrated just how "everyday" prayer is supposed to be by praying for a man who had become such a fixture at the city gate that people hardly noticed him any more as they passed by. They addressed a real-world concern in real-world language right in the middle of town, and as a result, thousands more people believed in Jesus that day (Acts 4:4).

God is good, all the time in every way. He is willing and able to meet the needs of his children if we will just ask. It is through our prayers that God can heal and speak. Though he doesn't need our help, he lovingly allows us to be part of the miracle of divine encounter. It is by grace that we can pray, and by grace that others can receive through our prayers.

FOUNDATIONS - WHY WE DON'T PRAY AT THE ALTAR

2

So why don't more churches do personal ministry? Why is it that the simple act of praying for people in church causes so much controversy and conflict? As I travel around the country, I often ask that question. And when pastors and leaders get really honest, these are the reasons they give:

1. "I'm afraid nothing will happen."

Many pastors automatically assume that the number of people who respond to an altar call is a direct reflection on their performance in the pulpit, and that feels risky. They fear the embarrassment they might feel if, after preaching their best message, they open up the altar for ministry and no one comes forward.

2. "I'm afraid something will happen."

It is impossible to predict exactly what will happen when the Holy Spirit is invited to work in people's lives, and many pastors are terrified of losing control of the service. When the script gets thrown out the window, they feel vulnerable and nervous. "What if too many people come to the altar, and I can't pray for them all? I'll never get home! What if someone gets emotional and makes a scene, or confesses to a horrible crime? The visitors might be offended. What if the same people come every week—the ones who just want attention or worse, the ones who have an agenda? I'll be like a sitting duck!" The idea of having to deal with the unexpected is more than some clergy can handle, so they tighten their grip on the order of worship to keep things safe and predictable.

> *Many pastors are terrified of losing control of the service.*

3. "We don't have an altar."

Not all churches actually have altars, and for some, this logistical hurdle seems too big to overcome. For example, in certain denominations, altar rails are not a traditional part of the sanctuary layout. Furthermore, thousands of churches, particularly new ones, meet in school buildings, offices and other rented facilities with little more for furniture than folding chairs. If there is no place to kneel at the front of the sanctuary, where can people come to receive prayer? The physical design of some worship areas makes the idea of altar ministry harder to picture, especially for someone who is already reluctant.

4. "It's an open invitation for flaky people who just need attention."

Unfortunately, personal ministry does seem to attract people who will want to pray for others as a way to meet their own needs for acceptance and significance. This is an inherent problem, because being a prayer usher carries with it a level of authority, responsibility and perhaps leadership. Prayer ushers are visibly set apart from the rest of the congregation and generally have been publicly approved of and commissioned by the pastor. Members of a body that may be emotionally unhealthy or have a strong need to feel important might leap at the opportunity to be included in such an exclusive group. And if they are allowed to pray and minister to others, they can potentially do more harm than good.

5. "I don't know how."

Many pastors have never seen what personal ministry looks like in a church service, so they simply have no concept of how to make it happen. Without some exposure to altar ministry, or at the very least, some good, informative materials, pastors lack the motivation and the tools necessary to organize and implement it in their own services.

6. "We don't have time."

This is a most common excuse, especially in large or growing churches that run multiple services on Sunday mornings to accommodate a maximum number of people. For example, with three services starting an hour and 15 minutes apart, pastors argue that they already have a hard time fitting everything in and shuffling

---

ILLUSTRATION

A woman drove into the parking lot of her church the Sunday following the death of her mother. She was still raw inside from the grief.

The pastor, aware of what she was going through, saw her drive up and went to the parking lot to meet her.

"I'm so sorry about your loss," he said, kneeling beside her car. "I know how difficult this must be for you. In fact, maybe it would be best for you to come back next Sunday, when you might not be feeling so vulnerable. I'm concerned that in your emotional state, you might break down in the service. And...well...it would be rather disruptive. Perhaps I can stop by this week and we can talk some more."

And with that, the pastor went back into the church, leaving the woman in her car, angry, confused and hurt.

DOES PERSONAL PRAYER MINIS-
TRY HAPPEN IN YOUR CHURCH
SERVICES? IF NOT, WHAT DO
YOU THINK ARE THE MAIN
HINDERANCES?

the people as they come and go. "Personal ministry," they say, "would take too much time, and it's too unpredictable. Our services would constantly be running over, and that would create havoc everywhere from the parking lot to the nursery."

7. "We've never done it before."

Change in most churches does not come easy. Traditions and rituals can be hard to let go of, and sheep can be downright stubborn. If a pastor can sell to those in leadership the importance of personal ministry, then he faces the even scarier task of introducing the idea to his people, many of whom would sooner run down the street in their underwear than get up and go forward in church. Mainliners especially tend to fiercely oppose anyone or anything that would attempt to move them from spectator to participant.

8. "It won't work."

Doubt is always a big hindrance to prayer. As crazy as it sounds, some pastors don't believe enough in the power of prayer to put it to the test. They reason, "What if someone's prayer doesn't get answered? What will they think of our church? Won't it make them turn away from God? Could they sue the church?"

This argument stems from a basic crisis of belief. Even though most church leaders would *say* that they believe whole-heartedly that God answers prayer, they get in a theological quandary over, "We all prayed for Sally Sue to be healed but she died anyway." They don't know how to deal with the fallout when God doesn't "come through."

9. "My people don't really need personal ministry."

This is denial, or the "happy church" delusion. Some pastors really don't want to know too much about their parishioners. They like believing that everyone is basically doing OK, and they would rather not stir up problems or issues that might reflect poorly on the church's image as a whole. While they might gladly pray for those who are sick or grieving, they would rather deny the realities of addictions, abuses, or secret sins among their members in order to protect their reputation. Pastors fear, "If that kind of information leaks out, people will start to gossip. We might start attracting the wrong kind of visitors."

10. "We don't want to condone sin."

Finally, I have heard some well-meaning, though misguided, Christians express concern that praying for sinners somehow communicates approval of their ungodly lifestyles. But blanketed in the guise of this spiritual "concern" are self-righteousness, judgmental attitudes, and an overall lack of grace. This line of thinking says, "Only those we deem worthy can receive the Lord's blessing and provision here. You have to get right if you want to get anything from God!"

We will address all of these issues as we work through the following pages together. But before we go any further, I think it is important that I clarify exactly what I am talking about when I refer to "altar ministry" or "personal ministry." Since the goal of this book is to challenge and train you in every aspect of praying for others, I want to define the experience by taking a look at what it *is*, and what it is *not*.

LIKE FINE WINE POURED INTO A JUG OF WATER, JESUS' WONDROUS MESSAGE OF GRACE GETS DILUTED IN THE VESSEL OF THE CHURCH. HOW RARE TO FIND A CHURCH COMPETING TO "OUT-GRACE" ITS RIVALS.
—PHILIP YANCEY

FOUNDATIONS - WHAT ALTAR MINISTRY IS

3

First of all, let me say that I am using the terms "personal ministry" and "altar ministry" interchangeably. I will use them both throughout the book because, though they describe the same basic experience, they each highlight a different domain.

Because of my pastoral background and my passion for local churches, I have a strong desire to see ministry start and flourish at altars on Sunday morning. As we saw in the first chapter, God wants to touch his people personally and he has established prayer as the vehicle to do that. However, altar ministry is just a prerequisite to the kind of personal ministry that should happen on a daily basis in grocery stores, living rooms, break rooms and restaurants. People sin in public, so certainly we should be able to pray in public. If we can get Christians comfortable with the idea of praying for others in church, they are more likely to take what they know out into their neighborhoods where the needs and opportunities for ministry abound. Ideally, altar ministry should come first, and should be a springboard to make personal ministry a way of life for every believer.

Thankfully, there are many churches today that are becoming houses of prayer—modeling effective altar ministries. Consequently, they are reaping the tremendous blessings that flow as a result of individuals being touched by God. In fact, all the church growth principles combined do not attract people as quickly as a viable altar ministry, because when God begins to move and people are healed and set free, the whole community notices. When the manifest presence of God is evident in your church, word spreads like wildfire and you will find yourself adding chairs to the aisles. Non-Christians especially take note of changed lives because they are so hungry for some-

> *All the church growth principles combined do not attract people as quickly as a viable altar ministry.*

thing real to believe in. Just look around. Do we not live in a society where everything God has to offer is passionately sought after in all the wrong places?

Simply put, personal ministry is one person praying for another. It is a *personal* human encounter through which God is able to *minister* to the needs of one of his children. It is grace in action, and it can happen at any time, in any place. Now let's take an in-depth look at what personal ministry at the altar of a local church really is:

1. Altar ministry is the compassion of Jesus released at a point of contact for a person's felt need.

"When Jesus landed and saw a large crowd, he had compassion on them and healed their sick" (Matthew 14:14).

"When he saw the crowds, he had compassion on them, because they were harassed and helpless, like sheep without a shepherd" (Matthew 9:36).

Jesus' compassion, noted here on two separate occasions by Matthew, was the Father's love in action. Being fully human, Jesus identified with the pain and struggles of the human condition.

When Jesus witnessed a funeral procession for the only son of a widow, Luke described how he empathized with the woman, "When the Lord saw her, his heart went out to her and he said, 'Don't cry'" (Luke 7:13). At another time, Jesus met a rich young man who wanted to know what he must do to inherit eternal life. When Jesus told him to sell everything he had and give to the poor, the young man hung his head and sadly walked away because he could not part with his possessions. But rather than condemn the man, Jesus "looked at him and loved him" because he understood the difficulty of his request and the turmoil it created in the man's heart (Mark 10:17-22). God's love for us, as it was expressed through Jesus, is emotional and passionate. He therefore relates to us in an emotionally passionate way.

Will we stir up problems when we open up our altars for

GOD WANTS TO MEET YOUR DEEPEST NEEDS. HE WANTS YOU TO SEE, KNOW, TASTE, AND EXPERIENCE HIM IN WAYS THAT SHAKE YOU TO YOUR CORE. HE LONGS FOR YOU FAR MORE THAN YOU LONG FOR HIM. HE STANDS READY TO REVEAL HIMSELF, ENFOLD YOU IN LOVE, SPEAK TO YOU WITH POWER, AND TOUCH YOU WITH GRACE. HE HAS WAITED FOR YOU—FOR THIS MOMENT. ARE YOU READY? —TRISHA RHODES

IF JESUS WERE TO VISIT YOUR CHURCH NEXT SUNDAY AND BE GIVEN COMPLETE FREEDOM TO CONDUCT THE SERVICE, WHAT DO YOU THINK HE WOULD DO?

ministry? Yes! But unless we stir them up, we can't get to them with the grace of Jesus.

When God touches someone, the meeting point of his love and the person's need is the point of contact. Oral Roberts describes what he discovered about point of contact:

> All power has a point at which you make contact. In your automobile you turn on the key or step on the starter, and the motor turns over. Or if you flip a light switch there is an instant contact with the powerhouse that causes the power to come singing through the wires to give you light.

> Any source of power you can name must have a point by which you make contact with it. The important thing is not the point of contact. The important thing is that you release the power.

Oral goes on in his book to give an illustration of how point of contact works:

> The point of contact sets the time. Now how? If I were to say to you, "I'd like to meet you."

> And you say, "Fine, Oral Roberts, when?"

> And I said, "Oh, any time."

> And you said, "Where?"

> And I said, "Oh, anywhere." You and I would never meet.

> But if I said, "I will meet you."

> And you said, "Where?"

> And I said, "In front of the United States Post Office in downtown Tulsa."

> And you said, "When?"

> And I said, "Tomorrow at 3:00," we would meet. We would be setting the time and place so that

all of our interaction would be used toward getting to that point at the appointed hour. You see what I mean? It's very important to set the time for anything you do. So the point of contact sets the time for the releasing of your faith.

For example, Mark 5 describes a healing encounter between Jesus and a woman who had been hemorrhaging for 12 years. As Jesus made his way through a crowd, the woman reached out and touched the hem of his garment and she was immediately healed. We are told that "at once Jesus realized that power had gone out from him" (Mark 5:30).

In this story, the woman's fingers touching the very edge of Jesus' cloak was the point of contact for the release of the Father's compassion. It was the point at which, because of her faith, his power was applied to her specific need.

> *The point of contact is the critical connection between a dark place that needs light and the power source.*

Be it a physical touch, or simply an existential moment when faith is released and God's hand moves in response, the point of contact is the convergence of the love of God and a person's felt need. It is the critical connection between a dark place that needs light and the power source.

Often, God applies his compassion to our felt needs in order to open our eyes to our deeper needs such as salvation, forgiveness, acceptance and guidance. It is our felt needs, or surface needs, that rule our daily lives, and we are often unaware of the spiritual needs that lie beneath. With patience and love, the Father meets us where we live—lost jobs, financial struggles, painful relationships, physical illnesses—in order to establish an inroad into our lives.

The Bible is full of examples in which Jesus met felt needs first, and then moved on to deeper needs. He met Zacchaeus' need for self-esteem (Luke 19:1-10); he met his disciples' need to catch fish (John 21:1-6); he met a beggar's need for sight (Luke 18:35-43);

ILLUSTRATION

During a missionary outreach to India, our music team had the opportunity to share the gospel one-on-one with many students following our concerts. One incident stands out in my memory.

I was talking about Jesus to a small group of inquisitive boys, when one asked me if all religions led to God. But when I began to explain that Jesus was the only way, God's compassion completely overwhelmed my heart. With tears streaming down my face, I stood speechless.

With wide eyes, the boys asked why I was crying. I told them that I had felt God's immeasurable love for each of them so strongly I couldn't contain it. The Holy Spirit fell in our little circle at that moment and the boys began to cry too.

Praying for them, the Spirit filled me with the most powerful infilling of the Father's compassion I have ever experienced.

—Tina Teykl Parish, member of missionary team called Celebrant Singers

 NOTES

and he met a hostess' need for wine at a wedding party (John 2).

God is practical! He understands human dilemmas such as poverty, humiliation, hunger and loneliness. He does not feel insulted or roll his eyes when we ask him to bring home a lost dog or help us find our keys. He is a compassionate Father who understands our every need, big and small.

Personal ministry is important because it is an invitation for God to meet needs and touch people in meaningful ways. When we pray for someone, we become conduits of grace through which the love of God can flow.

2. Altar ministry is an application of the "One-Second Principle."

God can do more in a person's life in one second than we could in a whole lifetime of analyzing and "helping." But he has to be given the chance. Altar ministry gives God the opportunity to accomplish his plans in the lives of his children.

God is willing; he is able; and he is good. Knowing these things about him will help us pray boldly and with confidence. Regardless of the need, God can, in a heartbeat, reverse, undo and recreate because he is the Lord Almighty. Problems that have lingered for years can be completely resolved with one touch of his hand.

Imagine how long it would take for men to build a corridor across the Red Sea. Or how many hours might it have taken to catch enough quail to feed three million Jews? I wonder how many hours of counseling Paul would have needed in order to change his mind about Christians. And I wonder how the best and brightest chemists in the world today would fare if asked to change water into wine.

In human terms, these tasks would be overwhelmingly difficult and complex. They could take years to complete. Yet God, in his sovereign majesty, accomplished them all *instantly* with little more effort than a word or a thought. The Bible is clear about his

GOD IS _____.
HE IS _____,
AND HE IS _____.

ability, "Now unto him who is able to do immeasurably more than all we ask or imagine..." (Ephesians 3:20). He is God, and he could reshape the universe as easily as he can heal a body or mind.

3. Altar ministry is a visible display of public prayer.

Although there is a dimension of prayer that can be reserved for the prayer closet, the Bible makes it clear to us that prayer, at times, needs to be done publicly. For example, the prayer Elijah prayed in front of the prophets of Baal and the Israelites was a critical turning point for the nation (1 Kings 18:36-37). When the people heard his prayer and saw God respond, they "fell prostrate and cried, 'The Lord—he is God! The Lord—he is God!'" (1 Kings 18:39). God used Elijah's bold prayer to turn the hearts of his people back to him.

In another dramatic moment, as Jesus stood in front of Lazarus' tomb on the verge of his last recorded miracle, he looked up toward heaven and said, "Father, I thank you that you have heard me. I knew that you always hear me, but I said this *for the benefit of the people standing here*, that they may believe that you sent me" (John 11:41-42, italics mine). Jesus didn't really need to pray out loud to wake poor Lazarus up. In fact, he had already commanded that the stone be moved from the tomb. It was almost like he had an afterthought, "Oh yeah, I have to paint the picture for these people or they might miss the point!" And so before he called Lazarus out, he prayed. Just like Elijah, he had to do it "for the record," so that God would receive the glory.

Jesus didn't do miracles just to help people; he did them so that others would believe and be saved. And remember he commanded us to do the same thing, "I tell you the truth, anyone who has faith in me will do what I have been doing. He will do even greater things than these, because I am going to the Father. And I will do whatever you ask in my name, so that the Son may bring glory to the Father" (John 14:12-13). Non-Christians need to see prayer happen so that when God answers, they will know he is the one true God and they will put their faith in Jesus.

QUESTION

HOW OFTEN DO YOU PRAY FOR OTHERS IN PERSON?

HOW OFTEN WOULD YOU LIKE TO?

WHAT KEEPS YOU FROM DOING PERSONAL MINISTRY MORE FREELY?

 NOTES

THE POWER OF HONOR IN PRAYER IS THAT WE PRAY GOD'S HEART. WE PRAY HIS WORDS, HIS FUTURE, HIS DREAMS AND DESIRES. OUR PRAYERS ARE ALL ABOUT HIS ABILITY, HIS PLANS, HIS PURPOSES. THE FOCUS OF OUR PRAYER IS NOT THE NEED, THE FOCUS IS HIM.
—FAWN PARISH

Ed Silvoso, in his book, *Prayer Evangelism*, points out the importance of public prayer. He writes:

> Paul also gave instructions to take our prayers all over the city: "I desire therefore that the men pray everywhere" (1 Timothy 2:8, NKJV). Everywhere means in every place in the city, not all over the church building. When Paul and his companions arrived in Philippi and went looking for a prayer meeting, where did they go? Down by the riverside—hardly a private place (see Acts 16:13). Later, Paul and Silas were thrown in jail, where they prayed out loud. How did the nonbelievers who were present respond? "And the prisoners were listening to them" (Acts 16:25).

Altar ministry gives prayer a very visible, public place in the worship service and equips believers to pray grace for their family members, friends and co-workers.

4. Altar ministry is the conduction of extraordinary grace by ordinary people to ordinary people in Jesus' name.

In the story from Acts 3 that I wrote about in the first part of this book, Peter and John come across a man lame from birth at the temple gate. Every day he would beg for money there, but on that day, he would get much more. Instead of giving the man gold or silver, Peter reached out and helped the man up onto his feet, saying, "In the name of Jesus Christ of Nazareth, walk" (Acts 3:6). And he did, for the first time in his life. In fact, he took off into the temple courts "walking and jumping, and praising God" (Acts 3:8).

As people saw the man bounding around the temple, they recognized him as the lame beggar, and they were amazed. A crowd gathered around the disciples, and Peter began to preach. Many were saved that day as a result of the miracle.

But also as a result of the miracle, the religious officials wanted to know, "How did you do that?" And Peter was quick to answer, saying something like, "Why are you so surprised? It wasn't me who healed the man, but Jesus. You remember, the one you killed on the cross that God raised from the dead? It was by faith and in his name that the man is walking" (Acts 3:11-16 paraphrased).

When we pray for someone, we, like Peter, are simply calling on the name of Jesus. We are not the source of power; we are just the conducting agent through which the power flows. In other words, we are conduits of grace, connected strategically to both God and the need. It is his grace that saves and heals because he is the source of all good (James 1:17; 1 Corinthians 1:28-31).

In the name of Jesus, we have his authority through the power of attorney. We have access to God (John 15:7-8, 16), and our requests are heard based on his righteousness (2 Corinthians 5:21; James 5:16). Based on Jesus' work on the cross, we have the right and the privilege to come boldly before the throne in prayer. All that we must bring to the altar is the willingness to intercede, faith in God and his word, and a humble heart (James 4:6, 10).

> *It doesn't matter who you are, how you feel, or what you say; Jesus is the one responsible for the outcome.*

That takes the pressure off! Help is in the name of Jesus and his track record, not anything we have to muster up. It doesn't matter who you are, how you feel, or what you say because Jesus is the one responsible for the outcome. You can and will be trained, but whether you are experienced in years of praying for people, or have never prayed for anyone in your life, it doesn't matter. You can be the conduit to impart God's grace.

5. Altar ministry maximizes God's manifest presence which is invited by corporate worship.

His word makes it clear—God likes to be worshipped. As our creator, he is loving and patient toward us, but also jealous for our affection. Emotional and passionate about us, his children, he is pleased when we thank him and praise him for all that he is and does, and reverently honor him as Lord. He loves it when we sing to him, proclaim his words or quietly and humbly rest before him.

I THINK THAT WHEN GOD HEARS HIS PEOPLE WORSHIPPING HIM AND GIVING THEMSELVES TO HIM, HE IS MOVED AND SAYS WITHIN HIMSELF, "I WANT TO GO DOWN AND HEAR MY PEOPLE WORSHIP AND ADORE ME. THEY ARE GIVING THEMSELVES TO ME AND NOW I AM GOING TO GIVE MYSELF TO THEM." —ROXANNE BRANT

 NOTES

We can shout, dance, pray or bow—it doesn't matter. He yearns for a love relationship with us.

That is why corporate worship is often such a powerful experience. It is a lovers' dance—the sweet, sometimes playful, waltz of a bride adoring her bridegroom, and he, filled with pride, lavishing her with affection. When we worship God, he moves in close and draws us into his arms for an intimate exchange. His presence is strong and reassuring. And it is in these moments that God's presence is often spontaneously made manifest in individual lives of the worshippers. Miracles happen when we worship God because he inhabits our praise (Psalm 22:1). John Wimber, founder of the Vineyard movement, says that it is as if God inverts a honeycomb over us, and many people are touched by "gracelets," or drops of mercy.

> *When we worship God, he moves in close and draws us into his arms for an intimate exchange.*

Altar ministry takes advantage of the special context created by corporate worship to usher people to the throne and allow God to do his work in their lives. It maximizes the moment so that God's purposes can be fulfilled in and through his children. As we declare his nature and remember his deeds, faith is stirred and strengthened. Ross Parsely, worship leader at New Life Church in Colorado Springs, says that "worship affirms who God is, and prayer releases what he wants done." They are a natural pair, worship and prayer, because each leads to the other, creating a healthy cycle of dependence and gratitude.

When Isaiah worshipped God in the temple (Isaiah 6), he saw God's glory and holiness revealed in a vision. "Woe to me," he cried, "for I am a man of unclean lips, ...and my eyes have seen the King, the Lord Almighty" (Isaiah 6:5). Then the Bible says that an angel flew toward Isaiah with a hot coal taken from the altar and touched his lips with it, saying, " your guilt is taken away and your sin atoned for" (Isaiah 6:7). The Lord touched Isaiah at the

point of his discovered brokenness and humility. At the same moment, he commissioned him to be his spokesman to Israel. As Isaiah worshipped the Lord, he had a life-changing encounter.

6. Altar ministry allows for a personal response to the gospel.

George Barna's research indicates that 50 percent of the people sitting in church on any given Sunday morning are unconverted. Although some may be regular church attenders, they have never been led in a salvation prayer. Of the other 50 percent, many need physical healing, freedom from secret sins, spiritual renewal or guidance. Yet in too many places, church is an activity to be watched, not participated in. People sit through an hour of worship and take in information, but leave unchanged and untouched at the point of their specific need.

Offering personal ministry during church gives people the opportunity to respond to the gospel—to act on what they have heard or experienced through the service. It's a chance for those who are ready to receive to put feet to their faith by making a physical declaration of their need or decision. "[God] rewards those who earnestly seek him" (Hebrews 11:6).

This is important, not because God needs to have us at the altar in order to work in our lives, but because he will not force us to receive what he has for us. He will wait for us to step toward him with an open heart. Contrary to what it may seem, receiving is active, not passive.

For example, how many times have you sat in church feeling very convicted about something in your spirit, only to dismiss it on the way to the car and not receive it into your life? You can choose to ignore the Holy Spirit's nudge. You can wrestle with him over the same issue for months or years without ever giving in. But when, at that moment of conviction, you get up and physically acknowledge the call by going to the altar, praying with another believer, or even simply kneeling at your seat, then you say "yes" to God and you begin to receive the work in your life. The

QUESTION

HAVE YOU EVER BEEN PRAYED FOR PERSONALLY BY SOMEONE? BRIEFLY DESCRIBE THE EXPERIENCE.

HAVE YOU EVER HAD A NEED MET THROUGH PRAYER, OR FELT THE PRESENCE OF GOD IN A VERY REAL WAY? WHAT EFFECT DID THE EXPERIENCE HAVE ON YOU?

 **NOTES**

body and the spirit are connected. You don't have to get out of your seat to say "yes" to God, it just seems to help. Altar ministry gives you the opportunity to do that.

7. Altar ministry glorifies God and builds faith as needs are met and individuals experience Jesus personally.

Someone described religion as people who have never experienced God telling people who have never experienced God about people who did experience God. What a poor alternative to a relationship with the risen Christ!

Christianity is to be experienced, not just learned about. It is more than just an historical tale with a spectacular ending. Why? Because Jesus is alive. When he was finished being dead, he got up, and he is the same yesterday, today and forever (Hebrews 13:8). The same Jesus that healed the sick, calmed the sea and fed the 5,000 is still full of compassion and love and mercy, and still wants to meet our needs. We can know him and interact with him in a personal way.

When you receive prayer and a touch from God in your life, you are never the same. Your whole perspective changes when grace becomes a personal experience. It is the difference between watching your favorite team play from a stadium seat and being allowed to participate in the game. Critical attitudes and disbelief fade and are replaced by empathy, understanding and appreciation for the game itself and for each individual player. Christianity looks different through the eyes of one who has felt the arms of Jesus.

> *Christianity looks different through the eyes of one who has felt the arms of Jesus.*

When the living Savior does meet a need, God is glorified. He was then and he is now. Jesus explained this to his disciples when he told them that a man blind from birth had been so in order that "the work of God might be displayed in his life" (John 9:3). When the lame beggar was healed by the city gate in Acts 3, he got incredibly happy about what God did for him and he let everyone in town know about it! He got his need met; God received glory.

Not only does it glorify God when prayers are answered and needs are met, it also generates faith in others. Jesus said, "Do not believe me unless I do what my Father does. But if I do it, even though you do not believe me, believe the miracles, that you may know and understand that the Father is in me, and I in the Father" (John 10:37-38). He knew that doubt and disbelief would trouble the human race, so he suggested that we build our faith on what we see him do in the lives around us.

Altar ministry is the threshold between a loosely knit group of people with common beliefs and a true community of believers. It is what weaves individual lives together into a tapestry that is the church as Jesus intended it to be.

FOUNDATIONS - WHAT ALTAR MINISTRY IS NOT

4

It is worth pointing out a few things that personal ministry at the altar is *not* intended to be, because I have seen it confused or improperly named in some places.

1. Personal ministry is not a sign of weakness.

If people in your church need prayer, it does not mean that your church is dysfunctional or spiritually weak. If you need prayer, it does not mean that you are dysfunctional or spiritually weak. Life is hard. God designed us to be dependent upon his strength and provision to get through it. He also gave us each other because he never intended us to walk out our faith in isolation.

Jesus told Paul, "My grace is sufficient for you, for my power is made perfect in weakness." Paul responded by saying, "Therefore I will boast all the more gladly about my weaknesses, so that Christ's power may rest on me. For when I am weak, then I am strong" (2 Corinthians 12:9-10). The strength of the church lies in our ability to embrace our weaknesses and depend on God. Public displays of prayer are pleasing to him.

2. Personal ministry is not counseling.

Praying for someone should never involve telling him what to do. Because if you have the answer to his need, then why bother God with it? Those doing personal ministry listen and pray. That's all. This is especially important in church settings where liability must be understood and respected.

3. It is not a show.

> *The moment that any kind of prayer ministry begins to focus attention on anyone other than God, it has gone askew.*

It grieves me to see personal ministry turned into a spectacle meant to glorify a particular person or group of people. True altar ministry is not a form of entertainment and should never be a source of pride. The moment that any kind of prayer ministry begins to focus attention on anyone other than God, it has gone askew.

Humility is the key to effective altar ministry. It is the safeguard that keeps us from counting heads or taking note of who comes and who doesn't. The response to ministry time has nothing to do with how good the preacher's sermon was or how inspirational the choir sounded. It is the work of the Holy Spirit. Personal ministry is an invitation for God to work, and he can handle the responsibility for the outcome.

4. Altar ministry is not focused or dependent on the pastor.

Good prayer ministry does not rely on the personality or leadership style of the pastor or worship leader. It can and should happen regardless of whom is in the pulpit. The pastor's job is to be sensitive to the Holy Spirit's leading, facilitate the invitation, and then step back and let ministry happen. He may also need to provide boundaries or redirect some interactions, but he is not the center of attention.

That's because personal ministry of this kind is carried out by ordinary people. Altar workers must be trained, yes, but they are regular members of the congregation, trained to pray for others. This takes the pressure and focus off of the pastoral staff. It also prevents people from coming forward for prayer just so they can get one-on-one attention from the pastor.

5. Ministry time during a worship service is not the time for major spiritual surgery.

Think of it as a lube job, not an engine overhaul. Some people have spent a lifetime absorbing evil thoughts and behaviors and may require more intensive, authoritative prayer for healing. They may need a team of intercessors specially trained in deliverance to effectively overcome the enemy's grip on their lives. Certain situations warrant privacy and time, and should really not be dealt with during a worship service. The enemy loves attention, and if he can't stop prayer from happening, he will settle for working

NOTES

ALTARS ARE THRESHOLDS—THE FOOTINGS OF A DOORWAY—BECAUSE HEAVEN'S POWER DOES NOT POUR FORTH FROM A GIANT GARDEN HOSE IN THE CLOUDS. IT OPENS ITS GRACE AND POURS FORTH OVER THIS PLANET THROUGH PEOPLE LIKE YOU AND ME WHO WILL FIND A PLACE TO MEET GOD, AND THEN KNEEL THERE AND KNOCK. AT THE DOORWAY OF HEAVEN WE FIND THE DOORS OF OUR BEING SWUNG OPEN TO GOD, PRIVATE QUARTERS UNVEILED, HEART SECRETS REVEALED, AND GOD'S LIFE-POWER RELEASED TO US. NONE OF US CAN EXPERIENCE THAT WITHOUT ALTARS.
—JACK HAYFORD

QUESTION

HAVE YOU EVER BEEN UNCOM-
FORTABLE IN A MINISTRY SET-
TING? WHAT MADE YOU FEEL
UNEASY?

havoc on a wonderful ministry time by causing a scene that derails what God might be doing throughout the sanctuary.

6. It is not the appropriate time to receive new members into the church.

Ministry time should not be mixed with other commitment times because this can cause confusion. Visitors in particular may be reluctant to go forward to receive prayer unless they feel totally free to do so without making a membership commitment or, worse, having to explain why they don't want to join the church to someone who has simply misunderstood their intent. Ministry time is for people to receive prayer. Period. If a person wants to make a commitment to Christ or to missionary service, great! But spiritual commitments only—issues of membership or money need to be handled at a separate time.

7. Altar ministry is not a commitment to solve problems.

Those who pray at the altar are not expected to provide money, jobs, advice, attention or any other kind of help or service. God's presence is the healing agent and he will provide the answers. I am not saying that prayer ministers can never give out of their own resources to meet someone's need. But those decisions should be made later, after more prayer and seeking, not at the altar when emotions are running high and vulnerability is at a peak.

8. Altar ministry is not a big deal!

Praying for people was the foundation of Jesus' earthly ministry and the core of the early church. It should be as natural a part of our worship services as taking an offering or giving a benediction.

FOUNDATIONS - PRAYER USHERS

5

Several years ago, as we were first endeavoring to learn and walk in personal prayer ministry in our own church, my wife was studying Revelation 1 when the Lord revealed to her something that changed her prayer life. She was struck by the idea that John could be transported "in the Spirit" into the very throne room of God where he received the spectacular vision (Revelation 1:10). She realized that she, too, could go before the throne of grace "in the Spirit" to carry her petitions to God. This is what she wrote about the experience:

> With this new and exciting concept of prayer growing in my heart, I began to pray for one of my family members who was struggling and had strayed far away from God. Every morning as I rose early to pray, I would quiet myself and begin to picture the beauty and majesty of the throne room of God. And as I held that picture in my mind, I would tell the Lord that I was bringing my sister Shelley with me *in the Spirit*.

> Shelley and I would just stand, quiet and still, in the presence of God, letting the water from the throne wash over us with the healing that was promised for the nations. I did not tell God about all the dangerous activities that my sister was involved in. I did not tell him what I thought he needed to do in her life. I just stood silently by her side as we faced the brilliant throne of God and soaked up his love for us.

> Then one morning a startling thing occurred that made me forever aware that God cares more about those for whom we pray than we do. And I learned that there is great power in praying in the Spirit and letting God be in control, rather than always feeling like we need to dictate to God what should be done for our "friend in need."

GIVE, AND IT WILL BE GIVEN TO YOU. A GOOD MEASURE, PRESSED DOWN, SHAKEN TOGETHER AND RUNNING OVER, WILL BE POURED INTO YOUR LAP. FOR WITH THE MEASURE YOU USE, IT WILL BE MEASURED TO YOU. —LUKE 6:38

As I began my prayer time, I began to picture the throne of God, and was so caught up in the love and warmth of that scene that I forgot to "bring" Shelley with me in the Spirit. However, after a few moments of soaking up the beauty of that throne room, in my mind's eye I turned to look slightly to my side and my sister Shelley was standing there with me! I got the distinct message from God that he had seen to it that Shelley was there, even though I had forgotten. Oh, what a feeling to know that God is always awake even when we slumber and are unaware of what we need to pray about.

As I prayed in this manner for my sister, I was simply an usher. I was a conduit for God's grace to begin to wash over my sister without any judgment or condemnation on my part.

This exercise of meditation releases us from the guilt of not getting a specific answer to prayer, overlooks our lack of eloquence, and is not dependent on our verbosity or volume. It does not require that we memorize scriptures about the throne room word for word. It merely allows us and those we pray for to soak up God's love.

QUESTION

Look up the following references. Who is the intercessor in each one?

Numbers 16:48

Luke 11

Numbers 14:13-20

Genesis 18

Matthew 26:39

Hebrews 7:25

James 5:16

That term "prayer usher" has been tucked in the back of my mind for years, but when I began working on this training manual, it resurfaced like a lost puzzle piece. It fit perfectly.

I like refering to those who pray at the altar as prayer ushers because it suggests, as my wife discovered, some very important things about our role and God's role in the intercessory prayer process. Webster defines an usher as someone whose job it is to "introduce" or "direct" people. We know them as individuals who escort us to our seats in theaters, churches, stadiums and other large venues. Ushers are never the main attraction, they are present only to help us find where we belong so that we can enjoy the event we came to see. Once we are seated, they sort of disappear.

 NOTES

A prayer usher's role can be understood in much the same way. Their job is to "usher" or escort those in need to God in prayer, and then back off and let the Holy Spirit do the work. Prayer ushers don't need to have the answers, they don't need to be spiritual giants, and they don't even have to completely understand the problem or the need. They only have to be willing and available to go along in prayer and agree in faith.

In Luke 11:5-8, Jesus tells a parable about what it means to intercede for someone. The story goes something like this: A man's friend shows up at his house in the middle of the night after a long trip. Since his refrigerator is empty, the man runs next door to his neighbor and asks for some food to offer his friend. His neighbor is asleep and isn't excited about getting out of bed, but because the man is persistent, the neighbor eventually lets him in and gives him as much food as he needs. Jesus makes it clear that the man's request is not granted because he is a good person or because he is someone important, but "because of the man's boldness" (Luke 11:8).

There are three people in this parable—the friend in need (the traveler), the friend in deed (the next-door neighbor) and the friend to intercede (the man). The "intercessor" is the one in the middle who connects the one with the need to the one who has the answer. He is the go-between whose boldness pays off (this teaching is derived from the book *Incense and Thunder* by Dudley Hall).

> *"We are intercessors when another's need becomes our own."*

In prayer, God is always the friend in deed because he always has the answer. And there are many in need who don't know where to turn. Prayer ushers are the go-betweens; they are the friends who intercede. Dudley Hall writes, "We are intercessors when another's need becomes our own. The man is not bothering his neighbor because he himself is hungry, but because someone has come to him and he has assumed their hunger as his own."

CARRY EACH OTHERS BURDENS, AND IN THIS WAY YOU WILL FULFILL THE LAW OF CHRIST.
DO NOT BE DECEIVED: GOD CANNOT BE MOCKED. A MAN REAPS WHAT HE SOWS.
—GALATIANS 6:2, 7

Just as in the parable, it is the boldness and persistence of intercessors that will move the hand of God. Jesus sums up the meaning of his story by saying, "Ask and it will be given to you; seek and you will find; knock and the door will be opened to you. For everyone who asks receives; he who seeks finds; and to him who knocks, the door will be opened" (Luke 11:9-10).

Prayer ushers are connectors, conduits of God's grace. They are not the source of anything. With one hand to heaven and the other hand on the need, they become instruments of healing, touching and encouraging those in need.

BUILDING THE TEAM

Because of the nature of altar ministry, the selection process for building a prayer usher team is important. The pastor may select a leader for the altar ministry and commission that person to select his or her own team, or the pastoral staff may select the initial team members directly.

While each church goes about the process a little differently, most screen potential candidates through personal interviews and then require training for those selected. The initial questionnaire and interview should focus on the ten qualifications listed below. Candidates who do not meet the qualifications may be invited to interview again after a period of one year.

SUGGESTED QUALIFICATIONS OF A PRAYER USHER

1. Actively pursuing personal spiritual maturity and holiness (1 Timothy 3:1-13; Titus 1:6-9)

2. Believer in prayer

3. Willing to submit to church leaders and policies

4. Trustworthy and respected among peers

5. Committed and available for training and ministry times

6. Active member of home church for at least one year

7. Emotionally stable

ILLUSTRATION

Our lay witness team had gathered for morning devotions. Normally we studied the Scriptures and then offered prayer for the church where we were working. We had grown close as a team traveling around and sharing our testimonies.

A young lady from our team and a close friend of mine got up and walked up front to our team leader, George Wickes, and began to cry. "I have cancer" she said. George immediately called for the team members to gather around her and lay hands on her to pray.

Although I knew the power of prayer, this thought stopped me in my tracks, "What if my faith for her healing isn't strong enough? God might not answer." Frustrated and confused, I stood in the back. How I *underestimated* the Spirit's abilities in me, and *over*estimated my own contribution to the process!

—Janet Goff, Prayer Point Press

 NOTES

8. Desire to see people come to Christ

9. Team player

10. Patient and caring with others

SUGGESTED QUALIFICATIONS FOR MINISTRY LEADER

1. Demonstrates personal spiritual maturity and holiness

2. Active member of home church for at least three years

3. Proven record of service in other church ministries

4. Exhibits excellent people and communication skills

5. Good leader and organizer

6. Able to work well with pastor and church leaders

7. Meets all other requirements for prayer ushers

Throughout Unit One, I have tried to characterize altar ministry and explain why it is so important in the local church and the body of Christ. In the next unit, I will focus on training those who will pray, and addressing specific issues that your pastor may face in starting this kind of prayer ministry.

NOTES

SAMPLE PRAYER USHER QUESTIONNAIRE

Today's date: _____

Name: _____

Address: _____

City: _____ Zip: _____

Phone (day): _____ Evening: _____

How long have you been a member of this church? _____

How and when did you receive Christ? _____

_____

_____

What other ministries have you been involved in at this church?

_____

Do you have any experience and/or training in praying for others?
Explain.

_____

_____

Can you commit the necessary time to training and be available at
least twice a month during services? _____

Use the back of this page to tell us briefly about yourself (family,
job, hobbies)

UNIT TWO - TRAINING

Training - The Personal Prayer Model

6

Though every prayer ministry opportunity will be unique, each encounter should contain four basic components: the interview, the intercession, the inquiry and the invocation. Following these four I's will help you stay focused and on track.

The Interview

The first step in any prayer encounter is the interview. It is important for you as the prayer usher to gather some information so that you can pray effectively.

Ask first for specifics—the person's first name and what they would like for you to pray about. Good listening skills during these initial moments can not be overemphasized. Look directly at the person instead of around the room. Make eye contact. Remember his first name so that you can use it as you pray and speak to him. Let your body language communicate attentiveness. An excellent listening tool is repeating back what the person says, like, "What I hear you saying is that you feel…." Keep in mind that you may be hearing one side of a story.

As the person is sharing his request with you, be listening not only for information, but also for the heart of the matter. What is his felt need? What might his real need be? Try to understand how he feels—put yourself in his place. I call this "compassionate identification," which means connecting emotionally to someone at the point of his or her need. Consider this passage from Isaiah:

> Surely he took up our infirmities and carried our sorrows, yet we considered him stricken by God, smitten by him, and afflicted. But he was pierced for our transgressions, he was crushed for our iniquities; the punishment that brought us peace was upon him, and by his wounds we are healed. …[He] was numbered with the transgressors. For he bore the sin of many, and made intercession

for the transgressors (Isaiah 53:4-5, 12).

This is a prophetic picture of what Jesus did on the cross. Pure and holy, the perfect lamb of God without blemish, identified with sinful man in every way, even unto his own horrible death. That is compassionate identification—Jesus feeling the pain of sins he did not commit and the anguish of his temporary human form. What amazing love he had for us!

As a prayer usher, in the same way, you must try to identify with the person for whom you are praying because this ministry is about loving people, not processing them. You must prepare your heart by praying, "Lord, let me feel this person's need and pray as if it were mine." You listen with the ears of Jesus. Compassionate identification is empathy, but at a deeper level, because it is based on the love of the Father, and not just your own experience or ability to understand.

> *"Lord, let me feel this person's need and pray as if it were mine."*

This process of identifying with the needs of others is what Paul was talking about when he told the Galatians, "Carry each other's burdens, and in this way you will fulfill the law of Christ" (Galatians 6:2). But unlike Jesus, we are not to bear the burden ourselves, we are to bring it to him in intercession.

THE INTERCESSION

As soon as you feel that you understand the request, simply ask the person, "May I pray for you now?" This question is important for several reasons. First, it is respectful and shows sensitivity to the person by asking her permission to start praying, rather than just launching out before she's ready. Second, it is a gentle but effective way to move into prayer and avoid a sharing time that becomes too long and emotional. While it's important to get the necessary facts and listen compassionately, it's also important to remember that the person has come for prayer, not just to "spill."

ILLUSTRATION

Just east of Worland, Wyoming, in the foothills of the Big Horn mountains, is an area known to the natives as the "Bad Lands." It is a vast stretch of hills and canyons where nothing grows. In fact, some people call it the "Dead Lands."

However the barren, forsaken appearance hides riches beneath its surface, where huge resevoirs of natural gas and oil lie.

Could it be that beneath the surface of pain and problems lie spiritual riches? Jack Taylor writes, "Our infirmities are the trumpets that call us to prayer. No miracle was performed in the Bible that did not begin in a problem. The greater the problem, the greater the solution."

 NOTES

People who are hurting can sometimes be prone to sharing more than necessary because it feels good to unload on a caring ear. But stay focused. When you have the basic facts, make the transition, "Can we pray?"

Finally, asking permission to pray gives the person who has come the chance to verbalize her desire to pray, and that is significant. When the person agrees to pray with you about the need, she is making a verbal confession—not a confession of sin, but a positive statement of agreement—that means, "I am willing to submit this situation to God and let him take care of it." Sometimes a person hearing herself say something like that can initiate a breakthrough because God honors a good confession (Romans 10:9-10). Our own words powerfully affect our minds and spirits.

With that in mind, as you begin to pray, you may want to invite the person to pray with you out loud, either repeating short phrases after you, or praying her own prayer. In some instances, it may be very helpful for the person to actively participate in the prayer as opposed to just listening. This is a judgment call, and may not be appropriate or necessary in every prayer encounter. But it is a good idea to keep in mind. Of course you can invite and encourage the person's participation, but don't push.

While there are many prayer models that you could follow, in this manual I am going to suggest that you pray "grace." The word grace is an acronym that can help you pray for any need using five key words or phrases: G – God's nature, R – the Righteousness of Jesus, A – Ask, C – Confidence, and E – Exaltation of Jesus.

First (G), determine what characteristics of God might relate to the need and pray from that frame of reference. Let God's nature—who God is—be the focus of the prayer time, not the problem. Praying the answer will encourage the person you are praying for, and will help draw his attention to the one who will provide. God is our healer, our redeemer, our creator, our comforter, our defender, our protector, our friend, and much more. Nothing

G - GOD'S NATURE
R - RIGHTEOUSNESS OF JESUS
A - ASK
C - CONFIDENCE
E - EXALTATION OF JESUS

NOTES

we face is too difficult for him and there is no problem that falls outside the realm of his ability to make right.

Next (R), pray with the assurance that you are being heard based on the righteousness of Jesus and his finished work on the cross (James 5:16). I will say it again, it is his credentials—certainly not ours—that enable us to go boldly to the throne, which is why we pray in his name. "In Jesus' name" is not just a formula we say, it is the scriptural basis upon which our prayers are heard, and a safeguard to help us pray in line with God's will. His name is our authority (John 14:13-14; 15:16) and access to the throne of God. Also when you "pray in Jesus' name," you have the power of attorney to bind the forces of evil at work (Mark 16:17-18) and bless with the promises of God (Luke 24:50-51), just like Jesus did. His precious name is our key to unlock heaven's door in prayer.

The "A" stands for ask. Even though God knows what we need even before we do, it is important to submit your requests in prayer through the power of the Holy Spirit (Matthew 7:7-11). Ask as specifically as possible. This paves the way for Jesus to be glorified when he provides the answer. As you pray, seek God's face and not just his hand. He likes to meet our needs, but we actually meet his need when we seek him just to know him. God yearns to be intimate with us, and it pleases him when we seek after him for himself.

I believe one of the greatest skills you can learn as an intercessor or even just in your own personal prayer life is the art of praying scripture. And it is a skill, which means it can be improved with intentional practice and repetition. The Bible is not just our guide for life; it is our prayer language. Beautifully expressive, rich in content and powerful in truth, the Bible represents the heart and mind of God. It is his word—*the* Word.

> *The Bible is not just our guide for life; it is our prayer language.*

When we pray scripture, we never need to worry about pray-

WHEN WE QUOTE GOD'S WORD TO HIM IN PRAYER, WE ARE SAYING THAT WE VALUE HOW HE THINKS. WE ARE HONORING WHO HE IS.
—FAWN PARISH

? QUESTION

LIST SEVERAL REASONS WHY
PRAYING THE WORD IS SO IM-
PORTANT AND EFFECTIVE?

1.

2.

3.

4.

5.

6.

ing the wrong thing, because it will automatically line us up with the will of the author. It creates *agreement* between God and us. And we can be confident, knowing that it has *authority* in the spiritual realm. The word of God is a powerful and effective weapon against the forces of evil.

As you petition the Lord on behalf of another, ask in prayer using the scriptures as your template. If possible, pray the Bible word for word, inserting the person's name. You can do this with individual verses, longer passages or even stories. For example, you might pray 2 Corinthians 5:17 over a new Christian who is dealing with guilt from his former life. You could pray the first sixteen verses of Psalm 139 with someone feeling lonely or abandoned by God. And the story of Daniel and the lions' den would be a good prayer foundation for someone whose faith is being tested.

There are many good "promises" books that list key scriptures under headings like assurance of salvation, grief, fear, healing, temptation, guidance and more. A resource like this, or one you make yourself, is a great thing to have on hand for personal ministry. You can use the suggested verses contained in this manual to start your own reference list. I recommend Evan B. Howard's book *Praying the Scriptures* for a more detailed teaching on this topic.

Having quick, easy access to several Bible verses that apply to common needs will give you confidence as a prayer usher. Don't give in to your religious ego that might try to make you think you have to have all the passages memorized. While you can't really know too much scripture, there is certainly no shame in consulting what the Bible says before you pray, especially if you are unsure. And there is no place for pride at the altar.

Of course, committing a few of your favorite prayer scriptures to memory is a good idea, and will help you feel ready to pray in any situation. If you are seeking God daily and hungering after his word, you may be surprised at how easily you will recall particular verses in the context of intercession. The Holy Spirit is

your teacher in prayer, and he will help you remember and bring to mind God's word as you pray.

The "C" in grace stands for confidence or complete trust. Once you have compassionately identified with this person, ushered her into prayer, and presented her request to God, then let go. Remember, you are just the conduit, not the source. Once you have prayed, reaffirm God's nature—that he is good, willing and able, and that he hears and answers when we pray. Agree with the person that her need is now in God's hands, and that he is at work to meet it and fulfill his best plan for her life. "Do not let your hearts be troubled. Trust in God; trust also in me" (John 14:1).

Finally, praise God that Jesus will be exalted (E) through the answer to this prayer. Thank him in advance for what he is going to do to meet the need. That Jesus be lifted up is the highest calling and the ultimate purpose of all prayer.

It is appropriate that we pray "grace" because it is by grace that we can pray and by grace that God hears and answers. None of us deserve the mercy and goodness of God, however, in his love he bestows it upon us anyway. "For it is by grace you have been saved, through faith..." (Ephesians 2:8). We pray grace because we have received grace.

THE INQUIRY

After you have finished praying, inquire about the experience. This inquiry is essential for several reasons: (1) It gives the person who received prayer a chance to redirect or follow-up on something that was prayed; (2) It encourages the person to be sensitive to what the Holy Spirit might have said to him, or what he might have felt as you were praying; (3) It reinforces that the burden of help is on the living God, not you; and (4) It provides you with immediate feedback about the prayer time.

Sometimes, even after listening carefully and compassionately to the request, you may miss the target. Or, as you're praying, a side issue may arise that needs further intercession. Questions may

PRAYING THE SCRIPTURES:

INSPIRES OUR PRAYER
ILLUMINATES OUR PRAYER
GIVES IMAGERY TO OUR PRAYER
GIVES INTELLIGENCE TO OUR
    PRAYER
ADDS INTENSITY TO OUR
    PRAYER
PROVIDES INTIMACY IN OUR
    PRAYER
—JUDSON CORNWALL

 NOTES

arise that need to be dealt with immediately or at a later time by someone else. Therefore, it is important to always ask a few questions such as, "Did you sense anything in particular while we were praying? Did you hear anything? Did an image or picture come to mind? What did you feel?"

These questions invite the person to listen for God's voice and tune in to what he might be saying or doing. Many people have never heard God speak to them, and when they do, it is a hope-giving, life-changing experience.

As a prayer usher, you can help your partner learn to hear from God simply by prompting him to listen. Remind him of how God may speak to him—in a mental image or memory, a scripture, a "sense," or words in his own mind. Also emphasize that God usually speaks simply, "It's okay," "I love you," "Don't go." Be patient with this part of the prayer encounter as you try to help the person discern the work and activity of God in him or in the situation. As a prayer usher, you never want to be in a hurry.

> *Remember you are just the usher; what is really taking place is between God and the person for whom you are praying.*

Remember you are just the usher; what is really taking place is between God and the person for whom you are praying. Therefore, encouraging him to hear God for himself is important. If you feel like the Holy Spirit reveals something to you as you are praying, share it with your partner, but then ask, "Does this mean anything to you?" or "Is God saying something to you about that?" Always point him to God, not yourself.

Inquiring of your partner after you have prayed not only helps facilitate his ability to hear God, it may also help you evaluate your own effectiveness in identifying with the need. That being said, you must understand that some results of prayer will be known immediately while others will be known later. You can pray on target with passion and still have the person say, "Noth-

As I teach people to listen to God, I have them ask him such questions as: "Father, would you mind telling me what you think of me?" Or "Father, how much do you love me?"

To a man in Ocala, Florida, God answered, "You are all the son I could ever want." To a young mother in our community, God replied, "You are worth more than you think. You are worth as much as I am."

—Peter Lord

ing. I didn't hear or feel a thing." And that's okay. Not seeing an instant miracle does not mean that you failed, or that you didn't pray long enough or hard enough. Sometimes we just have to wait to know, and other times we may never really know, the results of our prayers. But what we do know is that God always hears and always responds in line with his best.

QUESTION

DO YOU THINK WE SOMETIMES PRAY AS IF WE REALLY DON'T EXPECT GOD TO RESPOND? WHY?

Another question that you may need to ask is, "Do you need to *do* anything in order to appropriate God's provision in this situation?" or, "Is there any action on your part required to receive the answer to this prayer?" Just as a verbal confession is powerful, sometimes a physical action is necessary to trigger a breakthrough in the spiritual realm.

Jesus often instructed people to do something in order to confirm what he had done in their lives—get up, pick up your mat, go tell your friends, quit sinning. God may be willing to grant the person's request, but he may first need to speak forgiveness to someone, pay back a debt, or let go of some possession. The act of his will might play an important part in his appropriation of the answer. Again, it is best for you to pose the question and then wait for the person to respond. Resist the urge to play God by telling him what *you* think he needs to do.

God is real and alive. He is the unseen third party in any personal prayer encounter. Remember, he is the friend "in deed." When you intercede on someone's behalf, you are not just tossing up suggestions to the wind, hoping fate will make you look good. You are talking to a loving, living, all-powerful God who loves this person beyond comprehension. So expect God to respond in a discernable way. At the very least, consider it possible that he might, and don't be shocked when he does. If we act as if he is not there, then we miss the point of the whole exercise.

THE INVOCATION

The blessing of God holds significant power, and we as Christians have the authority to invoke such a blessing. In a sense, a

 Notes

spoken blessing gives to the one who receives it permission to see himself in a different light.

Close the prayer encounter by speaking a blessing over the person for whom you have just prayed. Regardless of what else has transpired, you want her to know that she is blessed and loved by God. You want to remind her that God will continue to work in her life even as she leaves the prayer place. Let the final thoughts she takes away from the moment be an encouragement for that day and the days to come.

PRAISE BE TO THE GOD AND FATHER OF OUR LORD JESUS CHRIST, WHO HAS BLESSED US IN THE HEAVENLY REALMS WITH EVERY SPIRITUAL BLESSING IN CHRIST. —EPHESIANS 1:3

GRACE PRAYER CARD

PREPARATION TO PRAY

Submit to God for compassion, wisdom and discernment.
Understand the importance of listening to them and him.
Believe God cares and hears (1 John 5:14-15).

PRAYING GRACE

G - God's nature
> Who is God in the light of the need?
> > The God of salvation (Ps. 27:1, 62:2; 1 Tim. 1:15)
> > The God of healing (Ex. 15:26)
> > The Father above (Matt. 6:9, 11:28-29)
> > The victor over our enemies (2 Tim. 4:18)

R - the Righteousness of Jesus (2 Cor. 5:21)
> What did Jesus do in light of this concern?
> Pray in his name based on...
> > His righteousness (Acts 3:16).
> > His ongoing, heavenly intercession (Heb. 7:25).
> > > Bind the forces of evil at work (Mk. 16:17-18; Acts 10:38).
> > > Bless with the promises of God (Num. 6:24-27; Lk. 24:50-51).

A - Ask
> Submit your request in the power of the Holy Spirit.
> > **A**sk specifically (Matt. 7:7-11).
> > **S**eek his face, not just his hand (Matt. 6:33).
> > **K**nock on an appropriate scriptural door:
> > > a story
> > > a chapter
> > > a verse

C - Confidence (Ps. 37:3, 31:14-15)
> Affirm that God cares and hears us when we pray.
> Agree that he is at work.
> Let go of the problem and let God take over (John 14:1).

E - Exaltation of Jesus
> Praise God that Jesus will be seen and exalted through the results of this prayer request (Rom. 8:28-32; Heb. 12:2; 2 Tim. 4:18; Ps. 37:5-6).

AMEN

Give thanks for the privilege of praying (Col. 3:24; 1 Thess. 5:18) and for the answer, seen and unseen (Phil. 4:19-20).

TRAINING - THE NITTY GRITTY

7

Now that we have established a basic model for prayer, there are several guidelines that need to be discussed to ensure that personal ministry goes smoothly. I already covered some of these ideas in detail, but they are so important that I feel it is appropriate to summarize them here in the context of other practical points.

1. Prepare yourself for ministry by praying. Ask God to purify your own heart and examine your motives. Seek the Holy Spirit's guidance and wisdom. Trying to minister to others when you yourself are spiritually depleted, or battling something like anger, can be detrimental, so use good judgment about your own readiness to pray. As a prayer usher, you should be disciplined about your own personal time with the Lord throughout the week.

Once you have heard the person's request, don't be afraid to pause for a moment in silence before you start to pray so that you can listen for any scriptures or impressions that the Spirit might be giving you. This takes a little practice, but you will hear if you listen, because the Holy Spirit is real, and helping us pray is one of his top priorities.

2. Listen attentively and identify with the compassion of Jesus. Good listening skills are critical for personal ministry no matter what setting you are in. Listen beyond the facts for understanding, and pray using the person's first name.

3. Make prayer a priority. This sounds obvious, but it can be easy to get so wrapped up in talking about the problem, that you never get around to praying.

4. Ask for permission to pray. Even though consent may seem like a given when someone comes to the altar during the ministry time, it is courteous and helpful to ask permission before praying. Prayer is an invitation for God to come into the situation, and in fact, he will only come by invitation. Even Jesus asked the question, "Do you want to get better?" (John 5:6). As a prayer usher, you can't push someone into God's provision for his life. You must invite them to walk with you to the throne of grace.

5. Be sensitive to gender issues. Prayer can be a profoundly moving event—emotions are released, pain surfaces, grace and compassion flow. Those involved may experience a special connection, even intimacy, as they sense the presence of God together. Therefore, some safeguards are recommended. Ideally, men should pray with men, women should pray with women, and couples should pray with couples. As a precaution, prayer ushers should be paired up into teams so that no one prays alone. Teams should consist of two (or three) men, two (or three) women or a married couple. Young people and even children can serve as prayer ushers as well, especially in praying for other kids.

> *As a prayer usher, you can't push someone into God's provision for his life.*

This team concept has many advantages: it creates a non-threatening accountability system; it reduces the risk of abuse or improper emotional attachments; it provides a natural setting for mentoring; it catalyzes the powerful principle of agreement in prayer; and it can temper or balance strong prayer personalities. Another benefit of team praying—while one prayer usher is praying for the person in need, the other can be silently asking for God's covering over the prayer time, for his wisdom and guidance, and for his will to be done. In other words, while you are interceding for someone else, your teammate would be interceding for you.

6. Be aware of personal hygiene. People tend to chuckle when I bring this up in a seminar, but it has to be said. Since personal ministry brings you into close proximity with others, cleanliness is truly next to godliness. Neat appearance and a bright smile should be standard equipment for prayer ushers. Be particularly aware of your attire, breath, and hands. Your clothes should be modest—no low necklines or see through material. Make sure your nails are clean and groomed, and that your teeth are brushed for

ILLUSTRATION

I was raised in poverty by alcoholic parents, and as a result wrestled with much shame and anger as a young man.

One afternoon several years ago, a counselor I was working with prayed for me as we talked in his office. He asked God to set me free from all the baggage from my past, and I began to weep uncontrollably. As the man was praying, the memory of hiding under the bed with my mom as bill collectors circled the house flashed vividly in my mind, along with the shame and humiliation that it always brought on me. But this time, Jesus was standing near the bed. He leaned down and reached out his hand, drawing me out to my feet. Then he wrapped his arms around me.

Through that prayer encounter, I was able to let go of the pain I had been carrying because I realized that Jesus understood.

—Terry Teykl

? QUESTION

A PHYSICAL POINT OF CONTACT IS NOT ESSENTIAL FOR INTERCESSION—OUR PRAYERS CAN AFFECT PEOPLE ACROSS TOWN OR EVEN AROUND THE WORLD. SO WHY DO YOU THINK JESUS SO OFTEN TOUCHED PEOPLE WHEN HE PRAYED FOR THEM?

HAVE YOU EVER ANOINTED ANYONE WITH OIL? HOW WOULD YOU FEEL ABOUT DOING THIS?

fresh breath. Also avoid heavy perfume or cologne. Think about it—in the closeness of personal prayer, visible cleavage, spinach in your teeth or dirt under your fingernails can be a significant distraction.

7. Be sensitive in choosing the appropriate point of contact. As previously defined, the point of contact in prayer is the convergence of God's love and a person's felt need. It is the point at which, because of faith, his power is released and manifested in a specific situation.

The point of contact may be an existential moment in time when the prayer of faith itself sets things in motion. It does not necessarily have to be a physical touch. However, placing your hand on someone as described in Mark 16:18, or anointing her with oil as described in James 5:13-16 are both very scriptural and natural ways to apply your faith to the person's need as you pray (see also Mark 1:31, 41; 3:10 and 5:41).

You may want to place your hand on your partner's shoulder, on her hands, or on her head. You can also target specific areas if applicable, such as placing your hand on her back if the need relates to back pain, or on her neck, ears or feet in the same manner. Obviously, you need to very sensitive about this and ask permission if you're not sure that the person is comfortable with being touched. Some people don't like the physical contact and you will need to respect that.

Anointing the person with oil is very similar except that you can place a small amount (one or two drops on your finger is enough) of oil on her as you pray. The forehead is probably the most common place to anoint with oil, but you can anoint any place that is appropriate to touch.

Let me emphasize that there is nothing magic or hyper-religious about anointing with oil or even laying your hands on someone as you pray. The oil possesses no mystical qualities or powers—I've used everything from vegetable oil to the scented anointing oils you can buy in Christian retail stores. This is done strictly as an act of faith in obedience to Jesus' instruction, and as a symbolic gesture representing the power and work of the Holy Spirit. And because the oil is not the source of power or healing, quantity is irrelevant. One drop is just as effective as a gallon.

8. Watch as you pray. This means you might need to pray with your eyes open so that you can monitor the person's response. Be alert to his emotional state, facial expressions, and physical signs of stress or anxiety such as flushing or sweating. If he needs to sit down or even lay down, help him to a chair or someplace that is not in the way of foot traffic. In this situation, stay with the person and continue to pray out loud or silently until he indicates that he's okay. Never leave a distressed person to go pray for someone else, regardless of how busy the altar may be.

9. Have necessary materials on hand. Your Bible, the GRACE prayer guide and your list of scriptures are important references for you to keep handy when you pray, especially while you are still building confidence in personal ministry. You may not lean on these tools as much as you gain more experience, but they are still nice to have when possible. Tissues and anointing oil are also helpful to have available when you pray just in case they are needed. If your church has a system for tracking what happens at the altar, then you will need to have the necessary forms to fill out when you finish.

And finally, it is nice for prayer ushers to have nametags so that people know who you are and can easily identify you. Some churches come up with a way to "mark" prayer ushers, such as with a special pin or different color nametag, so that they stand out. This delineation makes it clear that you have been intentionally trained and commissioned, which is good for everyone to know.

10. Know when and where to refer. Prayer requests that involve felonies, potentially dangerous situations or evil influences should be reported or referred to the proper person. Know your limitations. You are not a lawyer or a psychologist or a clergy person. And while confidentiality is of the utmost importance,

NOTES

IF A CHRISTIAN RETAILER IS NOT ACCESSIBLE IN YOUR AREA, YOU CAN ORDER SCENTED ANOINTING OIL BY CALLING ABBA ANOINTING OIL AT 1 (877) 2 ANOINT OR EMAIL ANOINTOIL@AOL.COM.

QUESTION

IF YOU ARE BEING TRAINED TO DO ALTAR MINISTRY IN A CHURCH SETTING, TO WHOM SHOULD YOU REFER THE FOLLOWING?

A NEW CONVERT:

SOMEONE YOU THINK MIGHT BE A DANGER TO THEMSELVES OR SOMEONE ELSE:

SOMEONE YOU HAVE REASON TO BELIEVE HAS COMMITTED A CRIME:

A POTENTIAL CANDIDATE FOR DELIVERANCE:

SOMEONE WHO DESIRES LONG TERM COUNSELING:

OTHER (SPECIFY):

there is no legal "professional-client" protection. If you learn of illegal activity or have good reason to believe someone may be in danger, you are obligated to report this kind of information. It is perfectly acceptable for you to *not* pray, and instead simply say, "I think we need to talk to the pastor about this," or whatever is appropriate.

On the positive side of this issue, when someone receives Christ for the first time or perhaps feels he is being called into Christian service such as missions, he needs to be referred to the proper person for follow-up. Other referrals might be made to established groups in the church, such as specialized support groups or home churches, for someone who needs prayer support over an extended time. Make sure you are familiar with the resources that are available and approved by your coordinator.

11. Be aware of current events. This is not an exhortation to know everything about everything, just a reminder that happenings in our cities, our nation and around the world do affect people's mindsets, concerns and attitudes. Whether we want to or not, we all live our daily lives against the backdrop of current trends and crises, so as a prayer usher, you need to have a functional awareness of what is going on around you. News stories that impact your life will probably impact others as well.

12. Know and respect your church's doctrine and policies. Theology regarding issues such as deliverance, anointing with oil and speaking in tongues varies from church to church, and you need to be fully informed about what is and is not considered acceptable. Honor these boundaries diligently. If you are in a private setting, respect the belief systems of those in the group, especially the one for whom you are praying. Avoid extremes that might derail the overall purpose and spirit of the encounter.

13. Pray scripture whenever possible. Since the Bible is God's word representing his heart on all matters, it is the most powerful prayer language we can offer. It keeps us in line with his will and focuses our intercession on the answer, not the problem.

14. If applicable, record or log your encounter and submit the information to your coordinator or pastor. Some churches keep no records of altar ministry, some keep limited records, and others keep more detailed records. What is best for your church will depend on the answers to such questions as: How many come for prayer each week? Can we handle the paperwork with integrity? How will records affect perceived confidentiality? Is time an issue? Your leader should inform you of the procedure you will follow.

LIST ANY CHURCH DOCTRINES OR POLICIES (I.E. DELIVERANCE, TONGUES, OIL) THAT DIRECTLY AFFECT ALTAR MINISTRY GUIDELINES.

I have included at the end of this section a sample form that can be used to record prayer encounters, or your altar ministry team might devise its own to suit your exact needs. Regardless, report forms should be as brief and easy to complete as possible, containing basic information such as the date, who prayed, the type of request, immediate results, and referrals made.

Although I understand some of the complications that accompany this kind of record keeping, there are several significant advantages to doing so. There are times when it is helpful to be able to recall or substantiate something that was said weeks prior. Also, information like this can improve future training efforts.

However, most importantly, over time, these simple records become a story of faith and a testimony to God's grace and the power of prayer. Just imagine what it would be like to have a book of all the prayers answered in your church—all the needs God has met and miracles he has performed in the lives of people. What a marvelous way to honor and glorify him; and what a powerful legacy to leave for future generations!

> *"If I were you" statements should never be part of personal ministry.*

OBTAIN WRITTEN COPIES OF THESE POLICIES OR RECORD THE INFORMATION AS INSTRUCTED BY YOUR LEADER.

15. DON'T offer advice or pass judgment. "If I were you" statements should never be part of personal ministry. As soon as you begin to "counsel" the person, you are not only flirting with danger, you are also denying God the opportunity to be God.

 NOTES

Instead, clothe yourself in the humility of Christ. If you have a humble heart, you will seek desperately after God, and not think so much of your own wisdom that you presume to know the answer to life's challenges. Guard yourself from praying "preachy" prayers that are really just opinions in disguise, like, "Lord, give Wanda the courage to leave her deadbeat husband...," or "Lord, reveal to Frank that he needs to forgive his boss so he can have peace...." Some Christians have mastered this technique as a way to impose their own ideas on vulnerable people in the name of prayer.

16. DON'T talk about yourself. If you find yourself in the position of praying for someone who is going through a difficult time that you have experienced, such as the death of a parent, a serious illness, or a divorce, it's okay to share this with him...*briefly*. It can create a powerful connecting point and build trust.

Don't expound, though, on the details of your situation. Remember your purpose and turn attention quickly back to God and the business of prayer. You might say something like, "Wow, I can really relate to the feelings you're sharing because I felt much the same way during my father's illness. How are you coping with those feelings? Let's pray about that." This lets the person know that you understand, yet keeps the interaction from taking a wrong turn. If you feel prompted to visit more with the person and build a friendship, make it a point to follow-up later.

> *The first time someone's personal problem becomes public knowledge, you will have a cancer of mistrust and anger on your hands.*

17. DON'T turn prayer requests into gossip. Breaching confidentiality is perhaps the single most deadly mistake in any kind of prayer ministry. The first time someone's personal problem becomes public knowledge because a prayer usher repeats it, you will have a cancer of mistrust and anger on your hands. That is why integrity

I THINK MODERN CHRISTIANS SOMETIMES CONFUSE THE CALL TO INTERCEDE WITH A CALL TO BE A MESSIAH. ALL OF US NEED TO BE NEEDED, BUT SOMETIMES WE FIND A PERVERTED JOY IN SO IDENTIFYING WITH OTHERS' PROBLEMS THAT WE BECOME ENTANGLED WITH THEM.
—DUDLEY HALL

is one of the most important qualities for a prayer usher to possess. Except for the cases which require referral for some reason, you should be extremely cautious about passing along prayer requests without the person's permission.

SAMPLE RESPONSE CARD

Prayer Usher(s): _____

Date: _____

First name(s) of person(s) who came for prayer:

_____

Did the person(s) receive Christ for the first time?

_____

Was any further referral made?   Yes   No

If so, to whom did you refer the person(s)?

_____

The prayer request related to: (circle one)

salvation   healing   fullness   freedom   other

TRAINING - THE TOOL BOX

8

My favorite store is Home Depot. I can walk up and down the aisles for hours, fascinated by the ingenuity of thousands of tools, each designed to make some job easier. Big tools, little tools, I love them all. With the right tool you can do almost anything.

I learned the value of the right tool early in life. As a young boy, I worked on motor scooters and cars. When I was in seminary on a very limited family budget, I overhauled two Volkswagen motors just to keep myself on the road. The right tool often meant the difference between success and failure.

I also learned that in some cases, the right tool made things possible that would otherwise have been impossible. In one of the first churches I served in a small rural community, there was a cotton farmer. One afternoon when I was visiting him, he took me out in his fields in an air-conditioned cotton picker. Having picked cotton by hand as a kid, I remembered how hot and tedious the work was. But that day, we rode along comfortably while the machine effortlessly harvested more cotton in an hour than anyone could have gathered in a whole week of hand-picking. The work the cotton farmer could have done under his own power was made hundreds of times easier and more efficient by that magnificent machine.

"In the same way, the Spirit helps us in our weakness. We do not know what we ought to pray for, but the Spirit himself intercedes for us with groans that words cannot express. And he who searches our hearts knows the mind of the Spirit, because the Spirit intercedes for the saints in accordance with God's will" (Romans 8:26-27). In other words, when you pray for someone, the Holy Spirit is on the scene to help you, making you hundreds of times more effective than you could be on your own.

SPIRITUAL TOOLS

The issues and problems in people's lives can be complex and overwhelming. At times they might seem insurmountable. Pain they have carried for years is entrenched in their lives, and it can be hard to know where to start praying. That is why you so desperately need the Holy Spirit's help. Not only does the Holy Spirit intercede for you as you are praying, he also supplies you with tools you need for the job. The tools are called the gifts of the Spirit, and they are given for the work of ministry, especially personal prayer ministry to others.

1 Peter 4:10 says, "Each one should use whatever gift he has received to serve others, faithfully administering God's grace in its various forms." Romans 12:6 tells us that we are all given "different gifts, according to the grace given us." These gifts are your tools—they are the abilities of Jesus inspired in you by the Spirit to bring people into salvation and fullness in Christ.

In the back of my truck I carry a red tool box. It goes with me wherever I go. Though most days I don't have any need for the tools, they are always within easy reach when I do. I have done many odd jobs for friends and sometimes strangers simply because I had the proper tools handy at the right time.

The Holy Spirit works in a similar way. He is with you all the time, living inside you to replicate the life of Christ in you. You do not need the gifts every day, but they are ready and available to you all the time. When you come across a need, the Master Craftsman will hand you the right tool to be applied in the precise moment of personal ministry.

> *When you come across a need, the Master Craftsman will hand you the right tool to be applied in the precise moment.*

It is important to understand that the gifts are not anyone's to possess as their own in order to get attention or promote some personal agenda. Yes, God seems to pour out certain gifts in some people's lives more than others. But, we shouldn't say, "She has that gift, but I don't," because that insinuates ownership and leads

QUESTION

READ THE FOLLOWING REFERENCES. RECORD WHAT EACH SAYS REGARDING THE HOLY SPIRIT'S ROLE IN OUR LIVES.

ACTS 1:8

ACTS 2:41 (PETER WAS "PUI," PREACHING UNDER THE INFLUENCE OF THE HOLY SPIRIT.)

ROMANS 5:5

ROMANS 8:26-27

JOHN 14:16-17

JOHN 16:7, 13

JOEL 2:28

✦ ILLUSTRATION

During prayer time at our Thursday night Bible study, I began to pray aloud for Steve. To be honest, I wasn't particularly close to Steve, so my prayers were not born out of deep love or concern but rather out of the thought, *Uh oh, someone better pray for Steve's need.*

Sometime during the prayer, passion took over. Because it was such a profound and rare experience for me, I can remember clearly what I was thinking and feeling throughout the prayer.

I recall that my spirit got so caught up in praying for Steve that I didn't even know what I was praying. I remember a strange, but pleasant sensation within my body and feeling my mind so riveted on the prayer it was like I was staring at the situation and couldn't pull away. About halfway through my prayer, an unusual thought entered my head: *I'm not praying; the Holy Spirit is praying within me.*

—Jonathan Graf, *Pray!* Magazine editor

to labeling. It also disregards the Holy Spirit's presence and sovereignty in our lives, and misrepresents him as a person. Being one with God, the Holy Spirit is the keeper and giver of every gift, and he issues them to us as needed to enhance our ability to minister Jesus to others. He owns them—he loans them, and he is an equal opportunity lender. We are simply privileged to use them at his discretion. They are for his glory and purposes.

This may seem like an unnecessary concern with semantics, but it is critical that we have a sound understanding of the source and purpose of the spiritual tools so that we can handle them with both humility and confidence. They

> *Spiritual gifts are the real and powerful abilities of Jesus inspired in us by the Spirit to do the work of ministry.*

are not merit badges of spirituality to be flaunted or compared; they are the real and powerful abilities of Jesus inspired in us by the Spirit to do the work of ministry. They enable us, in a truly amazing and exciting way, to partner with God as conduits of his love to others.

Although not everyone agrees completely on what all these tools are, most people look to Romans 12:6-8, 1 Corinthians 12:8-10, 28, and Ephesians 4:11 as biblical references. In the following pages, I will focus on eleven of these gifts that the Holy Spirit can give you to enhance your personal prayer effectiveness:

Diagnostic Tools – wisdom, knowledge, mercy, discernment

Power Tools – faith, healing, miracles

Finishing Tools – apostolic prayer, prophetic prayer, pastoral prayer, exhortation

THE DIAGNOSTIC TOOLS

Anyone who has done any type of handy work is probably familiar with several diagnostic tools—tools that help you assess the problem and determine the best way to proceed. Diagnostic tools can tell you where to drill, where to cut, how far to go, or what's inside. They give you information that you need to do the job right.

Wisdom

Wisdom is a diagnostic gift that I compare to a plumb line because it is necessary to help you shoot straight and avoid being misled. With all of the scriptures, information and experiences that you bring to a prayer encounter, you need the inspired help of the Holy Spirit to know exactly how to apply the relevant information in your "bank" to the specific situation for which you are praying. The Spirit can hand you this tool when you need to pray in the wisdom of God.

This is comforting to know, because God is already at work and intimately acquainted with the person's needs, and all you have to do is be surrendered to him as a willing vessel. He makes all your preparation go better. Wisdom is the ability to understand God's perspective on life situations and pray with insight that makes the difference.

Knowledge

The gift of knowledge is much like a stud finder, helping you to see things that are normally hidden from you. It can give you a visual picture of what's behind the sheetrock so that you know exactly where to hammer the nail.

The Holy Spirit is omniscient—he knows everything about everything in both the physical realm and the spiritual realm. Therefore, he can reveal to you selected pieces of information that you would never know otherwise, in order to help you pray on target. The information may come to you as a word or thought in your own head, or as a mental image similar to a snapshot. At any other time, it would seem completely random. But in the precise prayer moment when you are searching for direction, it will be amazingly "right" and clear. Although these insights are a supernatural revelation, they are given quite unassumingly in your own

TO ONE THERE IS GIVEN THROUGH THE SPIRIT THE MESSAGE OF WISDOM, TO ANOTHER THE MESSAGE OF KNOWLEDGE BY MEANS OF THE SAME SPIRIT..., TO ANOTHER DISTINGUISHING BETWEEN SPIRITS....
—1 CORINTHIANS 12:8

WE HEAR THE TERMS "GUT FEELING, HUNCH AND INTUITION" FREQUENTLY. HAVE YOU EVER EXPERIENCED ONE OF THESE COMPELLING "SENSES" WHEN YOU THOUGHT IT MIGHT BE THE HOLY SPIRIT SPEAKING TO YOU?

thoughts and senses. It is not spooky or weird; it is just one of God's ways of communicating with you.

I was praying for a woman one time who was having trouble sleeping, and the word "suicide" came to my mind. Because I knew the woman fairly well, it seemed so far fetched that I knew it was probably God's voice. Sure enough, when I mentioned my "holy hunch" to her, she confirmed that she had been tormented by thoughts of taking her own life, and so I was able to pray much more effectively for her to find peace and rest.

The first healing that Vineyard founder John Wimber ever saw also illustrated the gift of knowledge. He was praying for a woman when suddenly the image of a breast flashed in his mind. Being a man of God, the thought troubled him. But when he asked the woman if she had breast cancer, she confirmed it and was healed as a result of their prayers.

The gift of knowledge, like all the gifts, requires some practice and experience to use well. However, don't be afraid to try and miss. If you think God is speaking a word to you or revealing an image to you, simply say to the person, "I am hearing (seeing) the word (a picture of) _____. Does this mean anything to you?" If the answer is no, simply move on in the prayer time without making any more of it. The Holy Spirit is an excellent and patient teacher, and he will work with you if you demonstrate a willingness to try.

Mercy

Because image is important in our society, people often work very hard to hide their true feelings from others. Many who are wounded or hurting walk around with smiles on their faces in order to hide their pain. The gift of mercy is a specific kind of knowledge that enables you when you pray to see past the façade and detect pain in someone's life. It enables you to sense hidden suffering, and empathize with a compassionate prayer.

Helping someone uncover and let go of buried wounds is

often like unlocking the door to freedom and healing in her life. Unresolved hurt in a person's life—even a Christian's—can lead to bitterness, robbing her of the joy and fullness of life in Christ. Through the gift of mercy, you as a prayer usher can pray someone through the process of leaving the pain at the cross and moving forward with God.

A good example of this gift in action is in Acts 9 when Ananias was sent by God to pray over Saul. Since Saul had been openly and aggressively persecuting Christians, Ananias had every reason to give Saul what he deserved, at the very least a good lecture about his savage behavior. But instead, when Ananias met Saul, he laid his hands on him and prayed for Saul to regain his sight and be filled with the Holy Spirit (Acts 9:17). In response to the vision God had given him regarding Saul's conversion and calling, Ananias was a conduit of God's mercy toward the man who eventually became a radical preacher of the gospel and author of much of the New Testament.

Discernment

Discernment is another valuable diagnostic tool that can help you know what and how to pray. I would liken it to an alarm that sounds a warning when it detects something harmful in the air such as smoke or carbon monoxide. If we are walking with God, the Holy Spirit will sound in us an internal warning when we are in the presence of something or someone that is in opposition to God. This gift of discernment helps us know what is right and what is wrong—what is true and what is false.

The Bible tells us not to "believe every spirit, but test the spirits to see whether they are from God, because many false prophets have gone out into the world" (1 John 4:1). In personal prayer ministry, discernment may tell us that the person we are praying for is not actually saved, or that an evil influence is at work in his life. It is the tool that helps us "test the spirits" involved in the situation so that we might know if they are under oppression, be-

WE HAVE DIFFERENT GIFTS, ACCORDING TO THE GRACE GIVEN US. IF A MAN'S GIFT IS...ENCOURAGING, LET HIM ENCOURAGE; ...IF IT IS SHOWING MERCY, LET HIM DO IT CHEERFULLY. —ROMANS 12:6-8

 NOTES

ing deceived, or lying. Discernment is not only a diagnostic tool; it is a safeguard in our lives as Christians.

THE POWER TOOLS

I recently rented a power washer to clean my deck. You know how they work—you hook your ordinary garden hose up to the thing and presto! You have enough force coming out of the end of the nozzle to knock you off a ladder. How I know that is not really important.

I'm intrigued with the before-and-after difference created by such a powerful tool. Even areas that I didn't think were really dirty suddenly become dramatically cleaner as the jet stream of water penetrates the surface to wash away months (or years) of dirt. In fact, the process is so entertaining to me that I ended up cleaning the driveway, the sidewalk, the grandkids' fort and most of the house as well.

The Holy Spirit is your power source in personal prayer ministry (Acts 1:8). He has several tools that he makes available to you that can supercharge your ordinary, human abilities. I call these the power tools—faith, miracles and healing.

Faith

Eventually someone will come to you for prayer who spills out such a complicated web of pain and problems that you catch yourself thinking, "This really *is* hopeless. How in the world can I pray?" It is at that moment that you can rely on the Holy Spirit and the gift of faith to jumpstart your confidence in prayer. When you feel overwhelmed, he can infuse you with the same faith that raised Lazarus from the grave so that you can cut through the negative and offer a prayer of hope.

As a prayer usher, it is important not to walk by sight because the stories of sickness, failure, tragedy and grief can quickly discourage you without the Holy Spirit's help. The power tool of supernatural faith is necessary to pray with boldness and expectancy.

...TO ANOTHER FAITH BY THE SAME SPIRIT, TO ANOTHER GIFTS OF HEALING BY THAT ONE SPIRIT, TO ANOTHER MIRACULOUS POWERS....
—1 CORINTHIANS 12:9-10

NOTES

One summer I operated a bulldozer clearing land for additional income. A D-7 caterpillar is a powerful tool for moving anything in its path—trees, boulders, small houses. In the same way, faith moves mountains of bad news and bleak circumstances to clear the way for hope and anticipation that things can and will get better.

> *Faith moves mountains of bad news and bleak circumstances to clear the way for hope and anticipation.*

Miracles

The second power tool is that of miracles. Jesus promises us, "...anyone who has faith in me will do what I have been doing. He will do even greater things than these, because I am going to the Father. And I will do whatever you ask in my name so that the Son may bring glory to the Father" (John 14:12-13). The "things" Jesus refers to are the signs and wonders—the miracles—that he performed here on earth. Jesus routinely worked miracles, and he tells us to expect the same (Mark 16:17-18).

A miracle is an occurrence, brought on by the divine intervention of God, which clearly defies a natural law of the universe or a logically anticipated outcome. It usually results in a radical change that is visible by many and brings glory to God. A miracle could be the provision of needed finances, the safe return of a missing child, the restoration of a blown-up marriage, or the agreement of radically opposed sides of an issue. It may happen as soon as you pray, or later as God works out his plan.

Healing

Finally, the Holy Spirit can make available to us the gift of healing, which is a specific kind of miracle. Just as Jesus demonstrated God's ability to heal, you too can pray in his name for people to be made whole physically, emotionally or spiritually. In fact, one-third of Jesus' earthly ministry was spent healing the sick.

In Acts 14:8-10, Paul demonstrates how you as a Christian have power through the Holy Spirit to see people healed. In this

THE LAW OF PRAYER IS THE HIGHEST LAW OF THE UNIVERSE—IT CAN OVERCOME THE OTHER LAWS BY SANCTIONING GOD'S INTERVENTION. WHEN IMPLEMENTED PROPERLY THE LAW OF PRAYER PERMITS GOD TO EXERCISE HIS SOVEREIGNTY IN A WORLD UNDER THE DOMINION OF A REBEL WITH A FREE WILL, IN A UNIVERSE GOVERNED BY NATURAL LAW.
—B.J. WILLHITE

Do you believe that someone could be healed as a result of your prayers? Why or why not?

passage, a lame man sits listening to Paul preach the gospel, and as Paul catches the man's gaze, he knows that the man is believing for his healing. So Paul calls out to him, "Stand up on your feet!" And the man jumps up and begins walking.

At that precise moment, Paul's words and look became the point of contact for God to work his purpose in the man's life. It wasn't Paul who healed the man, but he was the conduit for God's love and mercy. In a later section of this workbook, I will offer you in-depth training on how to pray for healing since it is probably the single most common request you will encounter.

The Finishing Tools

In the final stages of building a home, tools are used to cut trim, paint, lay carpet and install fixtures. It is these finishing touches that make the home look polished and give it a uniqueness apart from others.

In personal prayer, you may need some finishing tools from the Holy Spirit's toolbox to help people see the big picture of meaning and destiny for their lives. As you intercede with someone, these gifts make you a vessel through which God can direct, encourage, lead and shepherd the person into the unique place he has designed for him. Your tools for the job are apostolic prayer, prophetic prayer, pastoral prayer and exhortation.

The traditional teaching on these particular gifts refers to them as offices in the church—apostle, prophet, pastor and exhorter—and this is how most people think of them. However, each of these offices can become operative as gifts during moments of individual ministry. In other words, as a prayer usher, there are times when it is necessary and appropriate for you to pray, for example, in an apostolic manner over someone, even though you are not an apostle.

Apostolic Prayer

Apostles are ground-breakers, initiators of new things. They typically herald an innovative message that opens the door to better ways and times for those in their care.

When you pray for someone in a manner that enables her to see her life and future in a fresh way, you are praying apostolically. This kind of prayer can be very comforting and will often dispel confusion. It is forward thinking prayer based on God's perspective of the person's life.

The Holy Spirit can hand you this tool without your own awareness. As you listen and pray with sensitivity and compassion, something you say may supernaturally trigger in the person a new insight or idea. It might shed light on circumstances that seemed random and chaotic, causing the picture to suddenly come into focus and make sense. Apostolic prayer generally produces excitement and anticipation for a new move of God (Isaiah 43:18-19).

Prophetic Prayer

Another type of forward thinking prayer is prophetic prayer, which usually stems from one or more specific visions or revelations that the Holy Spirit gives to you about the person's future. Prophetic prayer tends to speak more pointedly into a person's life situation than apostolic prayer, sometimes even including details that can only be revealed to you by the Holy Spirit. In this manner, it works together with the gift of knowledge.

The Holy Spirit can hand you this tool when the person for whom you are praying needs direction or confirmation about a decision. He might enable you to pray prophetically for someone who has lost hope in a particular situation or who just needs encouragement to keep going.

This gift can produce excitement and hope by previewing the wonderful things God has in store. However, it can also serve as a warning about impending danger or difficulty. Because it offers a glimpse into the future, it can be God's way of saying, "Stop. Back up. Don't go there!" It can be a safeguard to keep someone from straying too far away from God's will.

 NOTES

Both of these tools—apostolic prayer and prophetic prayer— remind me of a techno toy I have called a Global Positioning System, or GPS. Similar in size to a pager, GPS's instantaneously and continuously track your exact location through information they receive from several global satellites.

When I'm on an airplane flying across the United States, my GPS tells me precisely what I am looking at out the window (I can even zoom in on residential streets!), how fast we are traveling, which direction we are headed, how long before we reach our destination and much more. I often use it to help me locate my hotel or conference site, and I have found it especially helpful in navigating downtown areas where my sense of direction can be totally useless amid the tall buildings and narrow, one-way roads.

Through these prayer tools that focus into the future, the Holy Spirit operates like a GPS, offering direction, meaning and guidance. Through our prayers, he can reveal to people where they are and how to get to where they need to be. These finishing tools help people fulfill the unique calling of God on their lives.

> *These finishing tools help people fulfill the unique calling of God on their lives.*

In 1995, I made the decision to leave the pastorate to enter into full-time ministry as a prayer evangelist. However, I had not told this to my congregation because I was still waiting to hear from God about the timing of my resignation.

During this period of personal uncertainty, a musician named Phil Driscol was scheduled to appear at our church in concert. Before the service, as my staff and the band gathered in the offices to pray for the events of the evening, Phil spontaneously prayed over me something like this, "Lord, I thank you for the new work you are leading Terry into. As he launches out, bless him in every way. Grant him peace about the direction in which you are taking him. Amen."

IT WAS HE WHO GAVE SOME TO BE APOSTLES, SOME TO BE PROPHETS, SOME TO BE EVANGELISTS, AND SOME TO BE PASTORS AND TEACHERS....
—EPHESIANS 4:11

Wow! When someone prays in a prophetic or apostolic manner over you, it hits you like a 2x4. I knew that my prayer usher had read my mail and that God was confirming to me the vision he had been showing me for several months. Phil's prayer gave me peace about the transition and a renewed confidence that I was heading into an exciting new place in my ministry.

Pastoral Prayer

As you pray for people who are hurting or confused, you may at times feel a strong sense of responsibility or concern for someone. You may find yourself in a very nurturing or caring role, much as a shepherd tends his sheep. This is another finishing tool that is available to you for altar ministry, that of pastor or pastoral prayer.

While the office of pastor is a gift to the church, you can pray pastorally for someone with a profound sense of caring and oversight so that the person feels anchored and secure. Pastoral prayer bathes the person in the love of their heavenly Father, assuring him of his place in Christ. This tool represents the father heart of God in action.

Exhortation

Finally, the gift of exhortation is a tool that you may need as you minister in prayer. To exhort, according to Webster, is to urge strongly or admonish. It is similar to encouragement, but much more forceful a term. Barnabas was an exhorter in the Bible, and he played a big role in Paul's success early in his ministry.

When you use the gift of exhortation, you can pray with words of comfort, consolation, encouragement, and counsel to keep someone moving in the right direction. Exhortation is important because life is tough. Sometimes a person knows where he's headed, but when obstacles are thrown in the path and he gets knocked down, he needs someone to brush him off and push him on toward the goal. He doesn't need new direction, he just needs a Holy Spirit inspired shove.

 NOTES

PRECAUTIONS

These spiritual tools come with some precautions because with them come the risks and dangers that always accompany high powered equipment. They are one hundred percent safe and effective when used the way God intended, but unfortunately we are not always able to do exactly that. The skills necessary to use them take time and practice to develop, and sometimes we get careless. Misuse, abuse, jealousy and pride in the application of spiritual gifts can cause great harm and create an attitude of mistrust and rejection toward the whole idea. Irresponsible use of the spiritual gifts can even cause people to fear the Holy Spirit himself.

However, throwing out the tools is not the answer! We need them to minister the compassion of Jesus through prayer, and they are not the problem. All aspects of altar ministry or personal prayer ministry, including the use of spiritual gifts, need to be carried out with order and discipline.

A man in my church accidentally cut one of his fingers off one afternoon while using a handsaw in his garage workshop. He had been working all day and was tired. He got careless. We called together a group of men to pray for him as he was taken to the hospital for repair, and he eventually regained full feeling and movement. But as I sat in the waiting room, I imagined the headline in the paper the next day, "Man Cuts Off Finger with Handsaw—All Handsaws Banned." How ridiculous that would be! Yet that is exactly what we have done with some of the spiritual tools—banned them from use because someone got careless. What a tragedy.

In order to avoid spiritual injury, one important precaution that I have already mentioned is the understanding that the tools should never draw attention to themselves or the prayer ushers, but should always reflect honor and glory back to God through their results. Their function is to minister to the needs of people so that Jesus' name will be praised, not to say, "Look at me. Look what I can do!" If the focus is not on Jesus, red flags should go up.

Another precaution we can take is to keep in mind to whom

NOTES

the tools belong, and remember that we are completely dependent on the Holy Spirit for guidance in using them. We get in trouble when we think we own the gifts and we try to operate them without his help.

In order to build a house, many tools are needed, and sometimes they work together. In prayer, the gift of knowledge works alongside the gift of prophecy. Mercy can enhance healing and faith. Wisdom and discernment need to accompany exhortation. But just imagine how exciting and effective personal prayer can be when the right tools are used at the right time and God is glorified.

All of the gifts are available to us when we posture ourselves as the "friend to intercede" and pray according to scripture, trusting God for the outcome. The Holy Spirit inspires in each of us the abilities of Jesus so that we can be his "branches." We don't have to produce anything or make anything happen. We can just usher people to the Father in prayer and let the author of life touch their need.

ALL THE GIFTS WE RECEIVE IN PRAYER ARE INCIDENTAL AND SECONDARY TO GOD'S GIFT OF HIMSELF. —MAXIE DUNHAM

TRAINING - A WORD TO PASTORS

9

Wait. Don't skip over this section just yet. While you may not be a pastor, if you are reading this book, then you probably have one. And he or she is going to need your full support to put all this theory about altar ministry into action. In this section, I am going to speak very personally and candidly to pastors, as one who has already made the mistakes and seen the fruit of personal prayer ministry. However, I invite you to eavesdrop on the conversation so that you will better understand how to encourage and sustain your pastor along the way.

YOU ARE THE KEY

Pastor, you are the key to making altar ministry work. Although it ultimately should not be focused on you, it will never flourish without your stamp of approval. It will rise or fall based on your desire to see it happen.

I know a pastor who agreed, upon the urging of his prayer leader, to start a personal prayer ministry in their three church services. The prayer team trained some of the most trusted laypeople in the congregation to serve as prayer ushers, equipping them with material, special badges, the whole nine yards. But when the time came to make the invitation, the pastor got cold feet and the ministry never even made it down the runway.

I keep his picture in my Bible as a reminder that if a pastor is not sold out to an idea, any idea, it won't fly. Period. If you don't *really* want this to happen, all the training and preparation will be a waste of time. Once it's going, others will organize it, manage it, and take care of it. But you, and only you, can get it off the ground.

A PICTURE OF FREEDOM

I realize that anything that sounds related to what was once known as invitational ministry may be scary, because some of you have been offended by abuses in the past, and rightly so. We have all witnessed scenes of emotional manipulation from the pulpit, which resonated more like a hyped-up infomercial—"But wait...there's more!"—than a sincere invitation into the presence of God. It's ugly. But that's not what we're after.

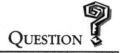

Picture something with me. Imagine your own sanctuary filled with people for a Sunday morning worship service. Imagine many of those people, from all over the room, slipping out of their seats and coming forward. Trained prayer ushers greet them, listen with compassion to their needs, and then simply ask God to touch them. You can hear the whispered prayers, a few sniffles, even some laughter. You sit back and watch as your people minister the grace of Jesus to each other. Let me tell you, it's a remarkable sight!

You see, there is no glitz. No hype. No manipulation. You won't need to prod or poke, coerce or convince. You need only to offer. Offer grace, compassion, love and concern. Offer Jesus through the personal touch of those who know him and will follow his example. Praying for people can become such a natural part of your service that it happens with as little fanfare as making announcements or welcoming visitors.

A young boy accepts Christ for the first time. An elderly man is comforted through a time of grief. A young couple brings their baby to be prayed for—she was born with a heart defect. A college student wants prayer to confirm the calling he feels to become a pastor. And none of those things would have happened if you had been unwilling to take the chance.

Now imagine this. It's 12:00 noon and the altar area is still scattered with people praying. So without disrupting the setting, you release everyone else to go with a benediction, and they slip quietly out of the sanctuary. You get in the car with your own family and head for lunch, leaving your prayer ushers behind to minister to people for as long as it takes. Some may even continue praying for several hours.

I know this is a radical concept for some of you to swallow;

79

 NOTES

especially those of you who feel like you must be in control all the time. But just think of the freedom that you could have as a pastor, if you knew that all good ministry in your church does not have to involve you. The burden to be everything to everyone can be lifted as you train your sheep to love on each other.

Do you want your people to build relationships and look to each other instead of you to meet all of their needs? Are you tired of feeling responsible for keeping everyone happy, making every hospital visit, spreading yourself so thin that you feel tired and emotionally depleted when you stand in the pulpit Sunday morning?

> *Multiply yourself in the form of trusted, spiritually mature prayer ushers who can be on call during your services and during the week as well.*

Jethro's fatherly advice to Moses is still good—teach your people to minister to each other. Moses' helpers spent time with the people so that Moses could spend time with God. It works!

Multiply yourself in the form of trusted, spiritually mature prayer ushers who can be on call during your services and during the week as well. Not only will you be preserving your health and sanity, you will be amazed at the results.

WHAT DO YOU EXPECT?

If I could counsel with you personally, I would ask you these questions. What do you expect to happen at church? What are your goals? Do you want to see new visitors every week? Do you plan your messages in the hopes that new families might join? Do you pray for a good offering?

I actually met a pastor once who took me into his office and showed me a file of 100 sermons, neatly arranged in order. He said that each Sunday, he went to the file, pulled out the next sermon and preached it. After two years, when he reached the end of the file, he would move to a different church and start over again.

TRUST IN THE LORD WITH ALL YOUR HEART AND LEAN NOT ON YOUR OWN UNDERSTANDING; IN ALL YOUR WAYS ACKNOWLEDGE HIM, AND HE WILL MAKE YOUR PATHS STRAIGHT.
—PROVERBS 3:5-6

Needless to say, he didn't expect much out of church.

If you are working toward bigger memberships and bigger budgets, you are light years ahead of that guy. It's good to reach new people and have money to pay the bills. But if that is as far as your sight reaches, I pray that something in this book will inspire you to a new and even greater vision. I pray that the Holy Spirit will burn into your spirit the revelation that your people really *want* to experience God in a personal way, and many of them *need* salvation, hope, healing or guidance. Ask God to give you a yearning to reap more than good attendance.

One night a good friend of mine, Dr. Mark Rutland, preached in my church. As always, his message was powerful, and at the end, he gave an invitation for people to respond. The altar filled.

After church I asked him, "Mark, what would you do if you opened the altars like that and no one came forward?"

"Hmm," he said. "I've never thought of that."

Oh that we would have so much confidence in the power of the gospel and the message of Jesus Christ—not our own abilities—that we would expect people to respond every time we preached it! Expect people to be healed and set free from sin and oppressive behaviors. Expect people to be convicted and saved. Train your prayer ushers to help you reap the response to a dynamic, living, life-changing gospel.

Personal ministry is the instrument that applies a two thousand year old message to the hearts and lives of your people today. With laser precision, it brings to bear all the truths of the Bible and the legacy of faith throughout the ages into a specific need or issue in a person's life. It's one thing for your sheep to learn about Jesus; it's another thing altogether for them to experience him in a personal and pro-

> *Personal ministry is the instrument that applies a two thousand year old message to the hearts and lives of your people today.*

IN THE BIBLE, AN ALTAR WAS A "HIGH" PLACE, NOT NECESSARILY GEOGRAPHICALLY, BUT SYMBOLICALLY. BECAUSE PHYSICAL PEAKS SUCH AS MOUNTAINTOPS WERE STRATEGIC WHEN FIGHTING AGAINST AN ENEMY, THE PEOPLE UNDERSTOOD AND HAD RESPECT FOR HIGH PLACES. THEREFORE, WHEN THEY WANTED TO HONOR GOD AND SHOW THEIR GRATITUDE FOR HIS PROVISION AND PROTECTION, THEY BUILT AN ALTAR TO SIGNIFY THE HIGH PLACE HE HELD IN THEIR LIVES. THEY WENT TO THE ALTAR TO PRAY AND MAKE SACRIFICES—IT WAS A SACRED POINT AT WHICH THEY COULD MEET WITH HIM. —TERRY TEYKL (*DOG*)

QUESTION

IS THERE A STIGMA OF ANY KIND IN YOUR CHURCH ABOUT "GO-ING FORWARD" TO THE ALTAR? IF SO, WHAT WOULD IT TAKE TO CHANGE THAT?

found way. Being prayed for transforms the gospel from theory to reality.

IT'S ABOUT CHRIST, NOT CRISES

Personal ministry is not just about solving problems. Don't let it live there or it will degenerate into an activity that quite frankly is depressing. I often teach that any time prayer becomes completely crisis-driven, it will eventually smother and die. Prayer that is motivated by who Christ is, however, will flourish.

Shape personal ministry as much around positive, quality decisions for God as around meeting needs. Deuteronomy 30:19-20 exhorts: "This day I call heaven and earth as witnesses against you that I have set before you life and death, blessings and curses. Now choose life, so that you and your children may live and that you may love the Lord your God, listen to his voice, and hold fast to him."

Encourage your people to choose life. Give them every opportunity to come to the altar and choose forgiveness over bitterness, righteousness over mediocrity, grace over judgement. You have members who want to give themselves to God in service—pray over them and consecrate their gifts at the altar for his purpose. Have people bring written notes of thanksgiving to the altar as an act of appreciation for the blessings of God. In addition, your prayer ushers can help people act on your message in some specific way so that they become doers of the word and not just hearers. You might call them to a special commitment regarding their families or finances, and some may want to seal their decisions at the altar.

In many churches, particularly traditional ones, the people tend to have preconceived notions that the altar is only for those who need to get saved or get right. "Going forward" is viewed as a sign of weakness or an admission of guilt and sin. You may have to chip away at these attitudes. Changing deeply rooted mindsets is not easy or quick, and I can only say be patient and persistent. Teach, mentor and model. Most will come around.

But here is the difficult word: If you lose some folks in the process, don't waiver; let them go. Don't sacrifice the ministry of Jesus over a few hardheaded nay sayers.

By associating your altar ministry with positive, healthy choices, you will lessen the stigma related to it and quiet the church gossips. Your people will learn, as you demonstrate personal ministry and gently guide them into understanding, that prayer at the altar is the essence of who Jesus was and is. It's about deepening individual's spiritual lives and growing closer as a church family.

THE DEAD SEA IS DEAD

The inland lake on the Israeli-Jordanian border is aptly named. At 1,286 feet below sea level, the Dead Sea is the lowest point on the face of the earth. The alkali level of the water is so high that basically nothing can live in it. Also known as the Salt Sea, the lake and its surrounding shores have been a source of salt mining since ancient times.

The reason that the Dead Sea is so black and lifeless is that although it has an inlet, the Jordan River, it has no outlet. The lake takes water in, but it has no way of letting it out. Since the water can't escape, it stagnates. Since it is not flowing, impurities, toxins and waste build up because they have no natural system by which to be filtered.

All living things need an outlet to be healthy. Your congregation needs to receive, but it also needs to give in order to keep from stagnating. And your people have so much to offer! John writes, "From the fullness of his grace we have all received one blessing after another" (John 1:16). Jesus underscores this by saying, "Freely you have received, freely give" (Matthew 10:8).

The prayer usher ministry is a prime outlet for the grace your members have received. When you look out over them, do you not see people you know have been healed, forgiven, set free, redeemed? As they are filled by the Holy Spirit and gifted for the work of ministry, they have a lot to give. Each of them has a

ILLUSTRATION

I was once called on to do the funeral of a very popular 18 year old young man. I didn't know the boy especially well, and his family didn't really have a church home.

In talking with the family, I learned that they were having to hold the funeral in a church 40 miles from their hometown because every other church that they called *refused to open their doors to non-members.*

As I stood up that day to try to bring comfort amid tragic circumstances, I looked out into the faces of more than 500 grieving, searching teenagers and many adults. I knew a large number of them were not saved. I took the opportunity to share the gospel message of life and hope, and I believe many heard it for the first time that day.

Those churches in Chris's hometown failed to recognize a God opportunity to demonstrate the love and compassion of Jesus.

calling and purpose in Christ and each of them, by grace and through prayer, can be a blessing to someone else in the journey.

Unleash them! Commission them to love and serve others out of their own abundance. Those who are more mature in the Lord are the ones to train first. And as they pray grace over the next spiritual generation, a beautiful cycle will emerge. Some will be ready to give; others will need to receive. Grace will flow through your church, bringing with it the life and hope we have in Christ.

In Matthew 14:16, the disciples wanted to send the hungry crowds away. But Jesus said no. Even though the disciples did not believe they had enough to give the people to eat, Jesus knew better.

Don't let your church just be a referral agency, sending people to this facility or that organization to get help. Give God an opportunity to meet their needs through your most valuable resource—your members. Give freely the prayer of faith in an atmosphere of abundant grace, and it will be given to you in the same measure.

PRAY AND GROW

As I worked on this book, I interviewed several pastors and prayer ministers of churches doing altar ministry so that I could share their testimonies. I always like to present a good cross section when I can, so I look for churches that vary in size, denominational affiliation, etc. The problem is, it's hard to find a small church that does good altar ministry, because the ones that do it well, grow. In fact, they usually grow exponentially.

Jesus balanced information with the formation of actual experience. He even said, "Believe me when I say that I am in the Father and the Father is in me; or at least believe on the evidence of the miracles themselves" (John 14:11). He revealed his Father not just through his words, but through signs and wonders. You can do the same by preaching the message of Jesus, and then letting your prayer ushers pray with people to validate the gospel content.

Word and deed ministry, as Jesus demonstrated in Matthew 4:23 (preaching the kingdom and then demonstrating the kingdom), renders a present tense reputation of Jesus in action that will attract people to him. In other words, when you pray for people and Jesus touches them, they go get their friends. Just look at the next verse: "News about him spread all over Syria, and people brought to him all who were ill with various diseases..." (Matthew 4:24).

> *"News about him spread all over Syria, and people brought to him all who were ill with various diseases..." (Matthew 4:24).*

As you pray for people and they experience the content of the gospel in the form of salvation, healing, fullness or freedom, others will be drawn to the manifest presence of God at work. They won't be able to help it. They may not even be able to explain it. You will hear people say, "I don't know why, but for some reason we just felt like we had to visit here this morning," or, "I've driven by this church many times, but today I felt compelled to come inside."

Good altar ministry is better advertisement than billboards, radio and television put together. That's not the motivation to do it, but it is unquestionably a result. Don't engage in personal prayer ministry if you are not prepared to deal with growth and visitors.

But these won't be typical church hopping visitors. I'm talking about unchurched visitors who may not understand common church etiquette, and who will sit in the place where Mr. and Mrs. So-and-so *always* sit, and who may not have the right kind of clothes to wear, and whose children may draw in your hymnals or be altogether disruptive! Yes, they will come because the Holy Spirit will woo them. The wounded, disenfranchised, outcasts of humanity will come to your doors because the needier they are, the hungrier they are for what God has to offer.

One night, a family visited my church, bringing their young daughter to be prayed for. Although she was fourteen years old, she weighed only 68 pounds and was very weak because she refused to eat. No one knew why, and medical and psychological

 NOTES

treatment had failed to help.

One of our prayer ushers prayed for the girl, who was curled up on the front row, and her family. In fact, the prayer usher was so moved by the girl's condition and the family's plight that she began making repeated visits to their home to pray. Gradually, the girl's appetite returned and she gained weight and strength. The family was so overwhelmed by the answer to prayer that they all accepted Jesus.

Praying grace will grow your church because people are drawn to the presence of God. Word will spread and people will come to your services just because they know they can receive prayer from someone who will listen to their story and offer compassion instead of condemnation. You invite him, and he will attract them. It's that simple.

TAKING IT TO THE STREETS

Pastor, as your congregation becomes more comfortable with personal ministry during church, you will notice something else. They will also be more open to praying for others at home or at work. After all, how can we expect them to pray for someone in the real world if we are too afraid to model it in the safety of God's house?

Encourage their boldness. You will be key in helping them apply their understanding in their daily lives. Offer the *Praying Grace* training to anyone who simply wants to learn to pray more effectively for friends and loved ones. If it's okay to pray at church, maybe they'll pray at Target or Burger King. If Jesus can meet needs at the altar, maybe he could do it in the hospital room or public school.

You could even start a marketplace prayer ministry as an extension of your altar ministry at church. For example, we have a *Box 3:16 Kit* that contains a prayer request box and all the necessary supplemental materials, including an instruction booklet. It equips individuals to target a local business in prayer. Also, Youth

MEETING THE FELT NEEDS OF THE LOST OPENS THEIR EYES TO THE REALITY OF GOD AND ALLOWS THEM TO MAKE A VITAL CONNECTION BETWEEN HIS POWER AND HIS LOVE FOR THEM (SEE MARK 1:40, 41; ACTS 4:9-12). MOST UNSAVED PEOPLE BELIEVE IN THE POWER OF GOD. THE UNIVERSE ITSELF IS CLEAR TESTIMONY OF GOD'S POWER. WHAT MOST OF THEM DO NOT BELIEVE IS THAT GOD LOVES THEM. WHEN GOD'S POWER IS RELEASED ON THEIR BEHALF, THEY ARE FINALLY ABLE TO MAKE THAT CONNECTION. —ED SILVOSO (*PERISH*)

with a Mission (YWAM) has successfully set up prayer stations on streets in New York City where people can stop and leave a prayer request or receive prayer on the spot. Dedicated prayer phone lines are another way to extend prayer to the marketplace. By implementing ideas such as these, you can pray grace over people in your community who don't go to church and don't know Jesus.

The testimonies from the prayer boxes and prayer stations confirm that many pre-believers are very open to prayer, and they become open to the gospel message as they sense the love of the Father. Prayer in the marketplace is an invitation for the Holy Spirit to infiltrate and influence your community, but prayer won't become a way of life for your people until it has become a way of life at church.

Pastors, make personal prayer ministry visible and viable in your church. Even if you have other prayer ministries like a prayer room or prayer cells, take advantage of Sunday mornings to demonstrate publicly the excitement and effectiveness of prayer. Your altar ministry can be like a wick to draw people into other prayer opportunities. The ability to go before the throne of God and present our requests, knowing that he will hear and answer, is such a privilege. Make it a priority.

If you are fearful, lay the burden of responsibility at Jesus' feet—he likes being in charge of the results. Don't miss out on what thousands of churches are discovering about the power of altar ministry. There is something so holy and special about watching your people intercede for each other; it is likely to become the primary focus of your worship services. Turn your people loose to pray, and don't be surprised when God begins to move.

PRACTICAL TIPS FOR IMPLEMENTATION

1. Start by praying at the altar yourself. Envision personal ministry happening as I have described. Write a brief, personal theology of prayer and intercession based on God's promises. Put it in a place where you can refer to it often. You might want to

QUESTION

WHERE DID JESUS DO MOST OF HIS PERSONAL MINISTRY? HOW DID THE GOSPEL MESSAGE SPREAD IN THE NEW TESTAMENT?

IN LIGHT OF YOUR ANSWER, WILL WE WIN THIS GENERATION TO CHRIST THROUGH SUNDAY MORNING SERVICES?

BRAINSTORM ABOUT POSSIBLE LEADERS FOR THE ALTAR MINISTRY:

NEW PRAYER USHER RECRUITS:

NAMES FOR THE GROUP:

give copies to your leaders, also. You must be sure about what you believe regarding prayer so that you will not be thrown into a belief crisis by circumstances, opinions, hearsay or personal feelings. Your foundation must be the word of God, not what you see.

Use these declarations to get you started: Jesus is alive. He was raised from the dead and took his seat in heaven with the Father (Acts 1:9). He lives to intercede for us (Hebrews 7:25). He told us to heal the sick and set the captives free (Luke 10:9; Matthew 10:1). The early church walked in the steps of Jesus, healing the sick and performing signs and wonders (Acts 3:6; 8:6; 9:34).

2. Share your vision with others in your leadership circle such as associate ministers, worship team members, elders and deacons. Study this material together. You might plan a visit to a church that is already doing altar ministry and ask questions.

3. Begin teaching and preaching on prayer. Share testimonies and information from the pulpit as well as in newsletters and bulletins.

4. Find a leader to oversee the ministry and give it a name.

5. Make a simple plan and allocate funds for training and materials.

6. Make a list of the first prayer ushers to be trained. Start small, focusing on members in good standing who already have leadership track records in the church. Develop an interview, screening and education schedule that works for your church. Begin seeing your members as ministers, ordained by the Holy Spirit and credentialed with the name and authority of Jesus. They are every bit as qualified as Peter and John the fishermen, Paul the tentmaker, and Lydia, who sold purple cloth. The Bible is full of examples of ordinary men and women with day jobs who became powerful ministers of the gospel.

> *The Bible is full of examples of ordinary men and women with "day jobs" who became powerful ministers of the gospel.*

7. If you don't have one, write a church policy that addresses issues such as deliverance or the use of various spiritual gifts in ministry. Your prayer ushers can only respect boundaries that are clearly stated and understood.

8. Explain the training process and the ultimate goal to the congregation so they know what to expect. Then commission the prayer ushers publicly and give them visible identification such as special nametags or badges. Only those who go through the training should be allowed to pray for others during the services, and you may need to reiterate this now and again to your congregation once you are started. By emphasizing this point, you will validate your prayer ushers, maintain quality control, and reassure your people that the altar ministry is being carried out with the highest level of integrity.

9. Designate a special Sunday to kick off the altar ministry. You might consider planning it in conjunction with some other special event like Mother's Day or promotion Sunday.

10. If your church does not have altar rails, simply designate a place for ministry to happen. If you have steps around the pulpit area, train your prayer ushers to come to the first step and stand facing the congregation. You can even establish the ministry area on the side or in the back of the sanctuary. The location is not important, so do what makes the most sense for your situation.

In some churches, people are taken to another room altogether for prayer at the close of the service. This not only alleviates many space and traffic problems, it is also a good solution for churches that have multiple services. At Church on the Way in Van Nuys, California, Pastor Jack Hayford actually has his people pray in small groups of three or four all over the sanctuary where they are seated. Another idea is to ask people who would like prayer to raise their hands, and have the prayer ushers go to them. Be creative. You don't even have to do it exactly the same way every Sunday, although I do recommend finding an overall pattern that works and sticking with it for the sake of consistency.

ILLUSTRATION

A pastor in a small church decided that the piano needed to be moved from the left side to the right side of the sanctuary in order to make room for a new pulpit that had been given to the church in memory of one of the founding members. So one evening during the week, he asked the building supervisor to move it. However, the following Sunday, the parishioners got so angry that the pastor moved the piano without their consent, that they voted him out!

A couple of years later, he was in the area and decided to visit his old church. When he went inside, to his amazement, the piano was on the right side of the sanctuary, exactly where he had moved it to. So he asked the new pastor, "How in the world did you get that piano over there?"

The new pastor replied, "Inch by inch."

ILLUSTRATION

I was teaching a prayer conference in a small Georgia city to a packed out downtown church. I wanted to demonstrate altar ministry and the importance of praying for salvation during one of the afternoon sessions. So, during the lunch break, I asked two people if they would play along by coming to the altar to receive Christ when I prompted them.

When we resumed, I taught on intercession and personal prayer ministry, and then began to model how a pastor on Sunday morning might invite people to the altar to receive Christ. I was thrown for a loop when, instead of my two stand-ins, *seven* people came walking down the center aisle and knelt at the altar.

I was the one who learned something that day—never assume that you know where people are spiritually. And never pass up an opportunity to invite people to know Jesus.

—Terry Teykl

11. If movement is a really new concept for your church, you may need to plan a progression of services centered around the altar leading up to your official kick-off Sunday. For example, a few Sundays in a row, you might bring specific groups (Sunday school teachers, youth, an outreach team) to the altar and let your leaders publicly pray over them. The prayer time can focus on a special upcoming project, event, or ministry opportunity of some kind. Do this several times to demonstrate what prayer at the altar looks like. Create the picture over and over so that it is no longer a mystery.

Next, you can invite your people to fill out a prayer request card in response to your message and simply bring it forward and lay it on the altar at the end of a service. Tell them the prayer ushers will take the cards and pray over them during the upcoming week. On several subsequent Sundays, use the same format with different emphases—have them write on a card a personal answer to prayer they have received, a special commitment they want to make, or a part of their life they desire to let God have. You get the idea. They can bring the cards to the altar and place them in a bowl, pin them to a cross, or hand them to a prayer usher. Just get them out of their seats and moving.

Finally, when you're ready to actually begin the altar ministry, don't rule out the possibility of planting ice-breakers for the first few weeks. Arrange for some of your prayer ushers to be available at the altar for ministry, while others actually come forward to receive prayer at your invitation. Sometimes all that is needed is for someone to go first. Years ago, when the altars would fill at the Billy Graham Crusades, the first ones down the aisles were always trained prayer counselors who were seated throughout the auditorium for the explicit purpose of breaking the ice. When the crowd saw several people get up to go forward, the flood gates would open.

You know your church. Don't throw them in the deep end if you know they can't swim. Ease them into the water by methodically removing as many obstacles as you can. Changing the spectator mindset is not easy, but it is possible with a little creativity and time.

12. If time is going to be an issue, either because of multiple services or other circumstances, meet with your leadership and determine how you will create the time the ministry needs. For example, prepare shorter sermons (and stick with them!). Print announcements in the bulletin instead of reading them all from the pulpit. Designate and prepare a room, close to the sanctuary if possible, where prayer ushers can take those who need more intensive or special ministry. This room is also your back-up in case the prayer time needs to overflow past noon. Do whatever you can to guard the ministry time, because you never know what God may be doing in the hearts of your people. He does not wear a watch and he is never in a hurry! Don't be tempted to forego.

13. When you open the altars for prayer, use music to help set the tone. Worship is the perfect atmosphere for altar ministry, and it gives those who remain in their seats something to do while others are praying. It also keeps the focus on God and not on who's going forward.

14. Meet with your prayer ushers before the service and tell them what you are preaching about, what response you hope to see, and any special invitations you will make.

15. Always keep in mind that the results of the invitation time are up to God, not you. He is responsible for the outcome. Set your focus on what he thinks about what you are doing, not what people think.

> *Set your focus on what God thinks about what you are doing, not what people think.*

16. Once you are started, continue to teach, inform and model. Take every opportunity to publicize answers to prayer and make the fruit of the altar time known.

QUESTION

LOOK BACK AT THE SECTION ENTITLED "WHY WE DON'T PRAY AT THE ALTAR." HOW WOULD YOU ANSWER EACH OF THESE OBJECTIONS BASED ON WHAT YOU'VE READ SO FAR?

1.

2.

3.

4.

5.

6.

7.

8.

9.

10.

 NOTES

17. Schedule *Praying Grace* training events quarterly, semi-annually, or annually to train new prayer ushers as you build the ministry. It is through this process of interviewing and educating that you and your leaders can screen any candidates that you feel shouldn't be in the role of prayer usher. With an established training procedure in place, any weeding out can be done in a sensitive and private way.

Unit Two has focused on many of the details of the prayer encounter itself, and of implementing the ministry of personal prayer in your church. In the third and final unit, we will be walking through four general categories of prayer requests—salvation, healing, fullness and freedom—and I will demonstrate how you can pray GRACE in each situation.

UNIT THREE - APPLICATION

APPLICATION - PRAYING FOR SALVATION

10

God is constantly at work drawing all people to himself (John 6:44). When the gospel message is presented, the Holy Spirit goes to work to convict people of their need for salvation. When your pastor invites people to receive Jesus Christ as savior, you can help guide them through this decision. It is the most important thing you can do as a prayer usher.

While some of you may have had some training in how to lead a person to Christ, many of you probably have not. It is not difficult or complicated, and there is no right or wrong formula. Your own explanation of the problem (we are sinners and therefore separated from God), the solution (God's love and Jesus' sacrifice on the cross), and our response (accepting his gift by inviting him to be our savior and Lord) will do the job.

However, just as a help to you, let me remind you of three of the most popular, tried and tested evangelism approaches as summarized by Elmer Towns and Neil Anderson in the book *Rivers of Revival*. These very succinct presentations of the gospel message of salvation may come in handy for you as you pray with someone wanting to receive Christ for the first time.

1. The Roman Road of Salvation

- Human Need   Romans 3:23

- Sin's Penalty   Romans 6:23

- God's Provision   Romans 5:8

- The Person's Response Romans 10:9

2. The Four Spiritual Laws

- God loves you and has a wonderful plan for your life.

- Man is sinful and separated from God; thus he cannot

ACCORDING TO GEORGE BARNA IN HIS BOOK *EVANGELISM THAT WORKS*, 50% OF CHURCH-GOERS TODAY ARE NOT SAVED.

know and experience God's plan for his life.

- Jesus Christ is God's only provision for man's sin. Through Him, you can know and experience God's love and plan for your life.

- We must individually receive Him as Savior and Lord. Then we can know and experience God's love and plan for our lives.

3. Evangelism Explosion

- Have you come to a place in your spiritual life where you know for certain that if you were to die today you would go to heaven?

- Suppose that you were to die tonight and stand before God and He were to say to you, "Why should I let you into my heaven?" What would you say?

Charlie Riggs, trainer for the counselors involved in Billy Graham crusades, suggests that the important thing to remember is that you are not presenting a formula, outline or systematic plan, but the person of the Lord Jesus Christ. As a prayer usher, escorting someone from death to eternal life is a profound privilege and reason to celebrate!

PRAYING GRACE FOR SALVATION

G – God's Nature

God is the God of salvation. His nature is always to love us and save us. He saves us from our sin and from death itself. Salvation was the reason for Jesus' life on earth.

- Our God is a God who saves... (Psalm 68:20).

- Help us, O God our Savior, for the glory of your name; deliver us and forgive our sins for your name's sake (Psalm 79:9).

- This is good, and pleases God our Savior, who

I PRAY THAT YOU MAY BE AC-
TIVE IN SHARING YOUR FAITH,
SO THAT YOU WILL HAVE A FULL
UNDERSTANDING OF EVERY
GOOD THING WE HAVE IN
CHRIST. —PHILEMON 1:6

 NOTES

wants all men to be saved and to come to a knowledge of the truth (1 Timothy 2:3-4).

- For the Son of Man came to seek and to save what was lost (Luke 19:10).

- Christ Jesus came into the world to save sinners... (1 Timothy 1:15).

Pray: Lord, we praise you because you are the God of our salvation. Your hand is stretched out to save _____ even now.

R – *Righteousness of Jesus*

God made the marvelous provision of salvation possible to us through the sacrifice of Jesus. In him, we can be righteous before God.

- God made him who had no sin to be sin for us, so that in him we might become the righteousness of God (2 Corinthians 5:21).

Pray: Based on your word, we believe that Jesus became sin for us so that in and through him, we can accept the free gift of right-standing with you.

A - *Ask*

Ask Jesus to come into the person's heart.

- Ask and it will be given to you; seek and you will find; knock and the door will be opened to you. For everyone who asks receives; he who seeks finds; and to him who knocks, the door will be opened. Which of you, if his son asks for bread, will give him a stone? Or if he asks for a fish, will give him a snake? If you, then, though you are evil, know how to give good gifts to your children, how much more will your Father in heaven give good gifts to those who ask him! (Matthew 7:7-11).

Because of the importance of this prayer, it is good for the

I AM NOT ASHAMED OF THE GOSPEL, BECAUSE IT IS THE POWER OF GOD FOR THE SALVATION OF EVERYONE WHO BELIEVES.... —ROMANS 1:16

person to pray the following out loud with you. Hearing themselves say this prayer out loud is a good confession.

Lead them to pray: Dear Father, I admit that I need you. Please forgive my unbelief and the things I have done wrong. I believe that Jesus is the Son of God and that he paid for all my sins with his death on the cross. I call on his name to save me. I now receive his life. I believe Jesus is living in me, that I am forgiven, and now I am a Christian. Because of this free gift of eternal life, I will go to be with Jesus when I die. Thank you Lord for saving me. [Note: A business size card with this prayer on it is available in packets of 100 through Prayer Point Press. Because this is such an important prayer in a person's life, we recommend purchasing the Sinner's Prayer Cards and keeping them on hand at the altar. When someone accepts Christ, you can give them one of these cards with the date on the back for them to keep in their wallet. They also make a great evangelism tool!]

- Yet to all who received him, to those who believed in his name, he gave the right to become children of God... (John 1:12).

- For it is with your heart that you believe and are justified, and it is with your mouth that you confess and are saved. As the Scripture says, "Anyone who trusts in him will never be put to shame. For there is no difference between Jew and Gentile—the same Lord is Lord of all and richly blesses all who call on him, for, "Everyone who calls on the name of the Lord will be saved" (Romans 10:10-13).

Pray: Jesus, I thank you that _____ has received you as his savior, because as many as receive you and believe on your name you give the right to become children of God. You are _____'s Lord! We know that God raised you from the dead and we are saved by trusting in you alone. Thank you that _____ has put his trust in you and he will never be put to shame.

ILLUSTRATION

On the second day of one of Mark Rutland's pastor's conferences in the midwest, a young man approached Dr. Rutland at the altar and asked for prayer. He shared that for some reason, every time Mark would start to preach, he would become so angry he had to leave the building. He had spent much of the conference sitting in his car.

As Mark began to pray, the man became very emotional, but Mark persisted until peace seemed to come over the man. Mark then asked him, "Have you ever asked Jesus into your life?"

"Well," the man replied. "I just finished seminary and I'm an ordained deacon in my church, but no one's ever really asked me quite like that before."

That young man had given so much to the church through his time, money and education. That night he finally gave Jesus what he had been waiting for all along—his life.

 NOTES

C – Confidence

God is the answer—the person's salvation. As a prayer usher, you are simply there to stand with them in prayer. Trust God to be the source.

- Trust in the Lord and do good; dwell in the land and enjoy safe pasture. Delight yourself in the Lord and he will give you the desires of your heart (Psalm 37:3-4).

- But I trust in you, O Lord; I say, "You are my God." My times are in your hands; deliver me from my enemies and from those who pursue me (Psalm 31:14-15).

Pray: Lord, we now trust you to forgive, save and work in _____'s life. We surrender to you for the workings of your great love.

E – Exaltation of Jesus

We want all honor and glory to belong to Jesus as a result of this prayer.

- To him be glory for ever and ever. Amen (2 Timothy 4:18).

Pray: Thank you for hearing our prayer, Lord. To you be the glory and honor forever. Amen.

If you are doing personal ministry at church, don't forget to record salvations that happen and report them to your coordinator or pastor for follow up. New converts need to be discipled and mentored, and there may be materials available to them to help them get started.

 NOTES

PRACTICE SWINGS #1

Read the following scriptures. Write out a prayer of salvation for someone named Amanda who wants to become a Christian.

G He will call out to me, "You are my Father, my God, the Rock my Savior" (Psalm 89:26).

R For if, by the trespass of the one man, death reigned through that one man, how much more will those who receive God's abundant provision of grace and of the gift of righteousness reign in life through the one man, Jesus Christ (Romans 5:17).

A For the grace of God that brings salvation has appeared to all men (Titus 2:11).

For God so loved the world that he gave his one and only Son, that whoever believes in him shall not perish but have eternal life (John 3:16).

C Therefore he is able to save completely those who come to God through him, because he always lives to intercede for them (Hebrews 7:25).

E "You are worthy, our Lord and God, to receive glory and honor and power, for you created all things, and by your will they were created and have their being" (Revelation 4:11).

 NOTES

 PRACTICE SWINGS #2

Dave has accepted Christ before, but he feels unsure about his salvation. Using the following scriptures, write out a prayer for Dave.

G He is our father in the sight of God, in whom he believed—the God who gives life to the dead and calls things that are not as though they were (Romans 4:17).

R But God demonstrates his own love for us in this: While we were still sinners, Christ died for us (Romans 5:8).

A ...for all have sinned and fall short of the glory of God, and are justified freely by his grace through the redemption that came by Christ Jesus (Romans 3:23-24).

He who did not spare his own Son, but gave him up for us all—how will he not also along with him, graciously give us all things? (Romans 8:32)

C But if Christ is in you, your body is dead because of sin, yet your spirit is alive because of righteousness. And if the Spirit of him who raised Jesus from the dead is living in you, he who raised Christ from the dead will also give life to your mortal bodies through his Spirit, who lives in you (Romans 8:10-11).

E Oh, the depth of the riches of the wisdom and knowledge of God! How unsearchable his judgments, and his paths beyond tracing out! Who has known the mind of the Lord? Or who has been his counselor? Who has ever given to God, that God should repay him? For from him and through him and to him are all things. To him be the glory forever! Amen (Romans 11:33-36).

APPLICATION - PRAYING FOR HEALING

11

If we are to follow Jesus' example, then we must pray for the sick, because, as I mentioned before, one-third of his earthly ministry was devoted to healing those who were afflicted in some manner. Matthew describes a situation that typified his friend and master, "When Jesus landed and saw a large crowd, he had compassion on them and healed their sick" (Matthew 14:14).

A person may need healing in his mind, body or spirit. Since physical healing in particular is the most common prayer request you are likely to encounter, it is important that you know what the Bible says about it, and that you are prepared to pray in this area.

This issue of physical healing is touchy for some and has spurned many theological debates. Each person's beliefs about it have been influenced by his church background and scriptural understanding, but often most strongly by his own personal experience. For that reason, some people are very passionate with regard to what they believe about healing.

With this in mind, I will encourage you to stick close to scripture as you pray for someone's healing. By praying the word of God, you are simply agreeing with what he has already said about the situation. Do not be anxious about the outcome; remember that God is responsible for the results, not you.

PRAYING **GRACE** FOR HEALING

G – *God's Nature*

It is God's nature to heal. Jehovah Rophi, meaning "the healer," is one of God's covenant names in the Old Testament. God is also good and incapable of being evil. He is good in every way, all the time. The New Testament amplifies another attribute of God's character—that of his Fatherhood. Jesus calls him "Father" over 100 times in the gospel of John alone. Furthermore, the Bible tells us that by the Spirit that dwells in us, we too can call

God "Abba Father," a very familiar term meaning "Daddy God." As our heavenly Father, God loves us beyond what we can imagine. Like an earthly father, he is concerned for our safety and well-being and would never be indifferent to our pain or suffering. We are his children and we can receive his healing touch.

- ...for I am the Lord, who heals you (Exodus 15:26).

- Then the Lord said: "I am making a covenant with you. Before all your people I will do wonders never before done in any nation in all the world. The people you live among will see how awesome is the work that I, the Lord, will do for you" (Exodus 34:10).

- Taste and see that the Lord is good... (Psalm 34:8).

- ...how God anointed Jesus of Nazareth with the Holy Spirit and power, and how he went around doing good and healing all who were under the power of the devil, because God was with him (Acts 10:38).

- Because of the Lord's great love we are not consumed, for his compassions never fail. They are new every morning; great is your faithfulness (Lamentations 3:22-23).

Pray: Father God, you created us and you know every detail about the inner workings of our minds and bodies. Thank you for making us your children and for being our "Abba Father." Your mercies are new every morning! I bring _____ before you Lord because she needs your healing touch.

R – Righteousness of Jesus

All healing is derived from the finished work of Jesus on the cross—he died for our sins and our sicknesses. So when we pray grace for healing, we pray based on Jesus' sacrifice. In him, we can be made whole just are we are made righteous.

- Surely he took up our infirmities and carried our sorrows, yet we considered him stricken by God,

I AM A PHYSICIAN DEDICATED TO HELPING PEOPLE FIND HEALTH AND WHOLENESS. THIS I WILL DO THE REST OF MY DAYS. WHEN I AM HELPING A PATIENT TO DISCOVER HIS OR HER OWN PATHWAY TO HEALING, I PRAY AND SEEK GOD'S WISDOM AND GUIDANCE. I MIGHT PRAY, "LORD, YOU KNOW ALL ABOUT MRS. JONES'S CONDITION AND WHAT IS NEEDED TO RESTORE HER BODY, MIND, AND SPIRIT TO COMPLETE WHOLENESS. I THANK YOU FOR SENDING YOUR HEALING POWER TO HER NOW. REVEAL TO US HER PATHWAY TO HEALING. SHOW ME THE SIGNIFICANCE OF THESE MEDICAL TESTS. QUICKEN MY MIND TO KNOW THE APPROPRIATE MEDICINES OR NATURAL THERAPIES TO COMBAT THE ATTACK AGAINST HER BODY AND BRING EVERY CELL, ORGAN, AND SYSTEM BACK INTO BALANCE AND HARMONY. DIRECT ME IN MINISTERING TO HER WITH EVERY POSSIBLE HEALING POWER, WHETHER THROUGH PRAYER OR MEDICINE OR NATURAL MEANS.
—REGINALD CHERRY, M.D.

smitten by him, and afflicted. But he was pierced for our transgressions, he was crushed for our iniquities; the punishment that brought us peace was upon him, and by his wounds we are healed (Isaiah 53:4-5).

- ...how much more will those who receive God's abundant provision of grace and of the gift of righteousness reign in life through the one man, Jesus Christ (Romans 5:17).

Pray: Jesus, you took up _____'s infirmities on the cross, and by your wounds she can be healed. Just as in you we can be considered righteous, I claim for _____ the healing and wholeness that you paid for so that she can reign in this life.

A - *Ask*

With the authority of the word of God, and in agreement with his heart, ask for the person to be healed. James 5:14-15 says, "Is any one of you sick? He should call the elders of the church to pray over him and anoint him with oil in the name of the Lord. And the prayer offered in faith will make the sick person well; the Lord will raise him up. If he has sinned, he will be forgiven."

As I mentioned earlier with regard to point of contact, anointing someone with oil is especially appropriate when you are praying for healing, based on this scripture in James. Using just a drop or two of oil on your finger, you might make the sign of the cross on the person's forehead as you pray.

As you interview the person, listen carefully as they share their request. Physical problems sometimes stem from spiritual ones, such as unforgiveness or bitterness. Ask the Holy Spirit to help you discern the real need. It is also important that you are sensitive to the person's level of faith in what they are seeking. Pray where they are and for what they are able to believe—don't pray your own agenda. For example, if someone comes asking for the courage and stamina to make it through chemotherapy treatments, don't pray off on a tangent, "God, I just ask that you heal all the cancer so this person won't have to take chemo at all!" Listen with compassion and pray in agreement.

- "But just say the word, and my servant will be healed." And his servant was healed at that very hour (Matthew 8:8, 13).

- Again, I tell you that if two of you on earth agree about anything you ask for, it will be done for you by my Father in heaven (Matthew 18:19).

- Then God said, "Let us make man in our image, in our likeness... (Genesis 1:26).

- Do you not know that your body is a temple of the Holy Spirit, who is in you, whom you have received from God? You are not your own; you were bought at a price. Therefore honor God with your body (1 Corinthians 6:19-20).

Pray: Lord, say the word so that _____ can be healed. Touch her _____ (fill in the area that needs healing, i.e. stomach, heart, nervous system, mind) and cause it to function like you intended. She is made in your image, and her body is your temple. She was bought at a price, and we ask you to apply your powerful work on the cross to her life and heal her.

C – Confidence

Our confidence in praying for healing must be firmly grounded in the truth of God's word and his desire to fulfill it (Jeremiah 1:12), not in our own personal experience. When a person forms his theology of healing based on what he has witnessed or been through himself, the result is a very limited and emotionally based belief structure.

God is so much bigger and more infinitely supreme than what one life can hold, that to put him a box defined by our own experiences is foolish. The reality that God does not always heal people to our satisfaction when we pray is not justification to stop praying for others to be healed. The truth is, many, many people have been healed; some have not. Accepting the death of a loved one is

ILLUSTRATION

Thank you Father God for teaching me how to read! The day started out with God's blessing and that day I was praying for Jesus to teach me how to read the Bible. I long to know his word because he is my life. Jesus talks to me all the time. He tells me what he wants me to do and I listen.

It happened during a weekend encounter at my church. Saturday night something happened to me and I was set free. Yes, I cried out to Lord Jesus to the depths of my heart and soul that night.

Later, I was talking to Carol, a lady in my church. I had called her on the phone and we started to read 2 Corinthians 5:17. Carol read first then she asked me to read and I thought help me Lord Jesus! I read like I had been reading always! Isn't that awesome? Now Jesus is teaching me how to use the Bible little by little. Thank you Lord Jesus for what you are doing in my life. I love you with all my heart, soul and mind.

—Barbara Buchanan, prayer seminar participant

 NOTES

difficult for us, but our mortality doesn't change who God is. We must trust in his sovereignty and his unchanging nature. The Bible says that he is able to do far more than we could ask or imagine (Ephesians 3:20), and in that truth lies the reason to keep asking and expecting healing for those who are in need.

- He sent forth his word and healed them (Psalm 107:20).

- Our Father in heaven, hallowed be your name, your kingdom come, your will be done on earth as it is in heaven (Matthew 6:9-10).

- I tell you the truth, if anyone says to this mountain, "Go, throw yourself into the sea, and does not doubt in his heart but believes that what he says will happen, it will be done for him. Therefore I tell you, whatever you ask for in prayer, believe that you have received it, and it will be yours (Mark 11:23-24).

- By faith in the name of Jesus, this man who you see and know was made strong. It is Jesus' name and the faith that comes through him that has given this complete healing to him, as you can all see (Acts 3:16).

Pray: We have asked in prayer for _____'s healing, and now we believe together that she will receive it. In Jesus' name and the faith that comes through him, we trust in what the Bible says and we put our confidence in God's promises for wholeness. We choose to listen to God and not to circumstances or people.

E – Exaltation of Jesus

Healing can be a powerful testimony to the glory of God. Just as the lame beggar who was healed at the gate Beautiful (Acts 3:1-10) and went "walking and jumping, and praising God" all over the city, people who have received a healing touch from God often attract attention! They are bold in testifying to his work in their lives. So as you pray for healing, you are praying for the name of

HE KNEW THAT THE PRAYER OF PETITION HAS A PART IN DEVELOPING OUR RELATIONSHIP TO GOD AND IN MATURING OUR SPIRITS. HE WANTS US TO BE HIS SONS, NOT ONLY HIS UNCOMPREHENDING LITTLE BABIES. THEREFORE HE HAS GIVEN US THE POWER TO CHOOSE AND THE RIGHT TO ASK.
—AGNES SANFORD

Jesus to be lifted up and magnified as a result of the work. He is worthy to be praised because he is the ruler over all the earth.

- Praise the Lord, O my soul; all my inmost being, praise his holy name. Praise the Lord, O my soul, and forget not all his benefits—who forgives all your sins and heals all your diseases, who redeems your life from the pit and crowns you with love and compassion... (Psalm 103:1-4).

- ...that at the name of Jesus every knee should bow, in heaven and on earth and under the earth, and every tongue confess that Jesus Christ is Lord, to the glory of God the Father (Philippians 2:10-11).

Pray: We praise you Lord, who forgives our sins and heals our diseases. You are a compassionate redeemer, and we worship and adore you. Amen.

ILLUSTRATION

A local newspaper in Lafayette, LA, *The Daily Advertiser*, published an article July 17, 2001 titled "Healing Rooms." It described the emergence of a ministry based on personal prayer for the sick. Here are some excerpts:

The "Healing Rooms of Wilmington" is part of a budding ministry based in Spokane, WA. It's expected to be in more than 150 cities worldwide by the end of the year.

After studying the prayer and healing practices of missionary John Lake, founder Cal Pierce opened the healing rooms to people of all faiths who wish to be prayed for personally.

The rooms operate much like a doctor's office. Visitors are greeted by a receptionist in a waiting area complete with soothing music and forms to fill out. Then they are escorted to a large room where teams of two or three people pray with them. Volunteers also pray in a separate room. About 30% of clients report physical improvement.

For more information, visit www.healingrooms.com.

 NOTES

 PRACTICE SWINGS #1

If you are in a class setting, do these practice swings with a partner, taking turns being the intercessor and the receiver. Take a few moments to prepare, and then pray for each other based on the scriptures given. When you have both prayed, offer feedback to each other. If you are working through this workbook on your own, simply write out the prayers or practice with a friend.

Situation: Sue needs healing for depression.

G Then will I go to the altar of God, to God, my joy and my delight. I will praise you with the harp, O God, my God. Why are you downcast, O my soul? Why so disturbed within me? Put your hope in God, for I will yet praise him, my Savior and my God (Psalm 43:4-5).

I lift up my eyes to the hills—where does my help come from? My help comes from the Lord, the Maker of heaven and earth. He will not let your foot slip—he who watches over you will not slumber; indeed, he who watches over Israel will neither slumber nor sleep. The Lord watches over you—the Lord is your shade at your right hand; the sun will not harm you by day, nor the moon by night. The Lord will keep you from all harm—he will watch over your life; the Lord will watch over your coming and going both now and forevermore (Psalm 121).

R I have told you this so that my joy may be in you and that your joy may be complete (John 15:11).

A And I pray that you, being rooted and established in love, may have power, together with all the saints, to grasp how wide and long and high and deep is the love of Christ, and to know this love that surpasses knowledge—that you may be filled

110

to the measure of all the fullness of God (Ephesians 3:17-19).

C   And I will do whatever you ask in my name, so that the Son may bring glory to the Father. You may ask me for anything in my name, and I will do it (John 14:13-14).

And without faith it is impossible to please God, because anyone who comes to him must believe that he exists and that he rewards those who earnestly seek him (Hebrews 11:6).

E   Let us fix our eyes on Jesus, the author and perfecter of our faith, who for the joy set before him endured the cross, scorning its shame, and sat down at the right hand of the throne of God. Consider him who endured such opposition from sinful men, so that you will not grow weary and lose heart (Hebrews 12:2-3).

Jesus Christ is the same yesterday and today and forever (Hebrews 13:8).

 NOTES

 PRACTICE SWINGS #2

Situation: Don is struggling with the fear of growing old and dying.

G And so we know and rely on the love God has for us. God is love. Whoever lives in love lives in God, and God in him. In this way, love is made complete among us so that we will have confidence on the day of judgment, because in this world we are like him. There is no fear in love. But perfect love drives out fear, because fear has to do with punishment. The one who fears is not made perfect in love (1 John 4:16-18).

R I tell you the truth, he who believes has everlasting life (John 6:47).

A Don't be afraid; just believe (Mark 5:36).

C This is the confidence we have in approaching God: that if we ask anything according to his will, he hears us. And if we know that he hears us—whatever we ask—we know that we have what we asked of him (1 John 5:14-15).

E Now to the King eternal, immortal, invisible, the only God, be honor and glory for ever and ever. Amen (1 Timothy 1:17).

Note: A good place to practice praying for healing is in a nursing home or a local hospital. There are always people in these facilities who do not have family close by and they usually welcome the encouragement and prayers of a kind visitor.

NOTES

APPLICATION - PRAYING FOR FULLNESS

12

Hopefully, personal ministry in your life and your church will not always center on problems or crises. It can be a time of great rejoicing, hope and excitement. That's because sometimes, people need to meet God at the altar just to ask for more of him, or to dedicate themselves to him for service, or simply to thank him and worship him in an active way. They may be responding to a powerful message or anointed worship, or to a yearning within for more of God. They don't have a problem; they just want to push beyond the familiar to encounter God in a new way.

The New Testament clearly shows us how people grew in grace and in the Spirit. For example, in John 20 the risen Lord "...breathed on the disciples and said, 'Receive the Holy Spirit'" (John 20:22). Then later he told them, "...stay in the city until you have been clothed with power from on high" (Luke 24:49). They encountered the Spirit again in the upper room (Acts 2:4), and again during corporate prayer following Peter and John's release by the Sanhedrin (Acts 4:31). The disciples were often filled with the Holy Spirit to equip them for ministry.

God frequently revealed himself in new ways to others in the early church as well. Paul went to a third heaven (2 Corinthians 12:2) and John received a revelation of Jesus (Revelation). Peter got a vision for spreading the gospel (Acts 10), and Mary listened for more (Luke 10:39).

None of us have all of God there is to experience. He is so vast and immeasurable that he can fill us, reveal himself to us, teach us and touch us every day that we are alive and still we would not know him completely. However, it pleases God when we seek after everything he has to offer. Paul wrote to the Ephesians, "Instead, be filled with the Spirit" (Ephesians 5:18). As a prayer usher, you can pray with people to walk in the fullness of Christ at a deeper level.

PRAYING GRACE FOR FULLNESS

NOTES

G – God's Nature

It is God's nature to reveal himself and be known—he desires that we know him deeply. He is exalted; he is worthy. He stands alone; there is none other like him. His voice can be like thunder or it can be a holy whisper. His thoughts are beyond ours and his ways are higher. He is indescribable in power and his love is beyond human comprehension. He is the great "I Am."

When someone comes to the altar to make a special dedication to the Lord or to experience more of him, you can open your prayer by declaring who God is and seeking a deeper revelation of his nature. As a prayer usher, you can invite the person to be open to what God wants to do in his life, even if it may seem new or different.

- O Lord, our Lord, how majestic is your name in all the earth! You have set your glory above the heavens. When I consider your heavens, the work of your fingers, the moon and the stars, which you have set in place, what is man that you are mindful of him, the son of man that you care for him? You made him a little lower than the heavenly beings and crowned him with glory and honor (Psalm 8:1, 3-5).

- For my thoughts are not your thoughts, neither are your ways my ways, declares the Lord. As the heavens are higher than the earth, so are my ways higher than your ways and my thoughts than your thoughts (Isaiah 55:8-9).

- Show me your ways, O Lord, teach me your paths; guide me in your truth and teach me, for you are God my Savior, and my hope is in you all day long (Psalm 25:4-5).

- The Lord confides in those who fear him; he makes his covenant known to them (Psalm 25:14).

IN SPITE OF OUR WEAKNESSES AND SINS, GOD HAS SET BEFORE US AN OPPORTUNITY TO DWELL WITH HIM IN HIS FULLNESS. IT IS TO THIS END THAT THE GRACE OF GOD IS WORKING IN OUR LIVES. —FRANCIS FRANGIPANE

115

 NOTES

Pray: O Lord, our Lord, how majestic is your name in _____'s life! You have crowned him with glory and honor. Show _____ your ways and confide in him because he desires to know you more intimately.

R - *Righteousness of Jesus*

Looking at Jesus, we see the nature of God revealed. The bread of life, the personification of true love, the source of abundant life here on earth—Jesus is our way to the Father. By walking the earth in human form, Jesus pulled back the curtain of the temporal to reveal the world of the infinite. In him we can receive the fullness of one blessing after another tethered by grace and sealed in truth.

- I tell you the truth, he who believes has everlasting life. I am the bread of life (John 6:47-48).

- On the last and greatest day of the Feast, Jesus stood and said in a loud voice, "If anyone is thirsty, let him come to me and drink. Whoever believes in me, as the Scripture has said, streams of living water will flow from within him" (John 7:37-38).

- Having loved his own who were in the world, he now showed them the full extent of his love (John 13:1).

Pray: Jesus, out of _____'s innermost being, let living waters flow and well up into eternal life. Draw near to him and show him the full extent of your love.

A - *Ask*

God promises to fill us if we ask him for the Holy Spirit. Just as the disciples received the Spirit on several occasions, we too can receive special anointings from God for service or personal growth. Moses is another example of one who earnestly sought after God to know him, and as a result, experienced him in a much deeper way than most. The Bible tells us that God spoke to Moses

THERE IS MUCH MORE OF GOD FOR US TO KNOW, AND MORE OF US FOR HIM TO HAVE. ONCE WE KNOW HIS REDEMPTION, WE BEGIN THE LIFELONG JOURNEY OF SEEKING HIM FOR ALL THAT HE IS. WE COULD CALL THIS PREVENTIVE GRACE, THE VACCINATION FOR PRIDE, SELF-IMPORTANCE, AND SPIRITUAL SATISFACTION, ALL OF WHICH KEEP US FROM GROWING IN HIM.
—TERRY TEYKL (*CAMP*)

face to face, as a man speaks to his friend (Exodus 33:11).

- ...according to your love remember me, for you are good, O Lord (Psalm 25:7).

- Ask and it will be given to you; seek and you will find; knock and the door will be opened to you. For everyone who asks receives; he who seeks finds; and to him who knocks, the door will be opened. Which of you, if his son asks for bread, will give him a stone? Or if he asks for a fish, will give him a snake? If you, then, though you are evil, know how to give good gifts to your children, how much more will your Father in heaven give good gifts to those who ask him! (Matthew 7:7-8)

- And this is my prayer: that your love may abound more and more in knowledge and depth of insight, so that you may be able to discern what is best and may be pure and blameless until the day of Christ, filled with the fruit of righteousness that comes through Jesus Christ—to the glory and praise of God (Philippians 1:9-11).

- What is more, I consider everything a loss compared to the surpassing greatness of knowing Christ Jesus my Lord, for whose sake I have lost all things. I consider them rubbish, that I may gain Christ.... I want to know Christ and the power of his resurrection and the fellowship of sharing in his sufferings, becoming like him in his death.... Not that I have already obtained all this, or have already been made perfect, but I press on to take hold of that for which Christ Jesus took hold of me (Philippians 3:8, 10, 12).

Pray: You are a good God who is willing to give us your very best. In Jesus' name, I bring _____ before you so that you can touch his need for more of you. I am asking, seeking, and knocking on _____'s behalf. Just as a father provides for his son, how much more will you give of yourself to him at his re-

ILLUSTRATION

A woman who attended one of our prayer conferences sent me this in an email. She wrote this verse to describe what it meant to her to meet God at the altar:

So she rocks in the arms of her Father,

the light of His love shining on her face.

Though others may glimpse her flesh and her sin,

she cares not as she stays in His embrace.

She sees through the eyes of her Daddy

all that He means her to become.

No longer held back by what was revealed,

but encouraged as she knows where to run.

—Steph Berganier, prayer seminar participant

117

 NOTES

quest? He wants to know Jesus Christ and the power of the resurrection. He is not fully there yet, but _____ is pressing in to take hold of that which you have called him for. Amen.

C – *Confidence*

We know that Jesus wants us to experience complete fullness in him, and to walk in his abundance every day. So you can ask him to fill you again and again, and then live in expectation that he will do it. It may be at the altar; it may be in the car on the way home from church; or it may be later during a moment of quiet reflection. Regardless, you can wait with anticipation, because he will reveal himself to you in a new and meaningful way.

- Now to him who is able to do immeasurably more than all we ask or imagine, according to his power that is at work within us, to him be glory in the church and in Christ Jesus throughout all generations, for ever and ever! Amen (Ephesians 3:20-21).

- This is the confidence we have in approaching God: that if we ask anything according to his will, he hears us. And if we know that he hears us—whatever we ask—we know that we have what we asked of him (1 John 5:14-15).

- Come, Lord Jesus (Revelation 22:20).

Pray: By faith, we receive a new measure of fullness for _____ in his walk with you. Even now, come Lord Jesus and fill him.

E – *Exaltation of Jesus*

When God fills us in a new way, it is always for the purpose of strengthening our relationship with him and building the body to bring glory to the Son. He does not pour out his Spirit on us to elevate us in any way. Seek to be filled with a humble heart so that you might be equipped for more effective ministry to others.

- The Spirit and the bride say, "Come!" And let

WHEN GOD LOOKS UPON MY LIFE GRAPH, HE SEES NOT JAGGED SWERVES TOWARD GOOD AND BAD BUT RATHER A STEADY LINE OF GOOD: THE GOODNESS OF GOD'S SON CAPTURED IN A MOMENT OF TIME AND APPLIED FOR ALL ETERNITY. —PHILIP YANCEY

him who hears say, "Come!" Whoever is thirsty, let him come; and whoever wishes, let him take the free gift of the water of life (Revelation 22:17).

Pray: The Spirit and bride say to _____, "Come, your thirst shall be quenched." Thank you, God, for knowing _____'s heart and his desire to press in to you. The water of life is your free gift to him now and forever! Amen.

 NOTES

 PRACTICE SWINGS #1

If you are in a class setting, pray over these two situations with a partner, taking turns being the intercessor and the receiver. Take a few moments to prepare, and then pray for each other based on the scriptures given. When you have both prayed, offer feedback to each other. If you are working through this workbook on your own, write out the prayers or practice with a friend.

Situation: Last week, a little boy was brought to the altar for prayer and he was healed. As a result, the entire family has come to the altar this week wanting to receive a blessing and more of God in their lives.

G Praise the Lord, O my soul; all my inmost being, praise his holy name. Praise the Lord, O my soul, and forget not all his benefits—who forgives all your sins and heals all your diseases, who redeems your life from the pit and crowns you with love and compassion, who satisfies your desires with good things so that your youth is renewed like the eagle's (Psalm 103:1-5).

R Praise be to the God and Father of our Lord Jesus Christ, who has blessed us in the heavenly realms with every spiritual blessing in Christ. In him we have redemption through his blood, the forgiveness of sins, in accordance with the riches of God's grace that he lavished on us with all wisdom and understanding (Ephesians 1:3, 7-8).

A The Lord bless you and keep you; the Lord make his face shine upon you and be gracious to you; the Lord turn his face toward you and give you peace (Numbers 6:24-26).

C Now faith is being sure of what we hope for and certain of what we do not see. And without faith it is impossible to please God, because anyone who

comes to him must believe that he exists and that he rewards those who earnestly seek him (Hebrews 11:1, 6).

E Now to the King eternal, immortal, invisible, the only God, be honor and glory for ever and ever. Amen (1 Timothy 1:17).

 NOTES

 PRACTICE SWINGS #2

Situation: A young Christian couple that you know has just had their first baby and they are elated. They want to dedicate themselves, their new son, and their marriage to God.

G Forget the former things; do not dwell on the past. See, I am doing a new thing! Now it springs up; do you not perceive it? (Isaiah 43:18-19)

Every good and perfect gift is from above, coming down from the Father of the heavenly lights, who does not change like shifting shadows (James 1:17).

R You are worthy, our Lord and God, to receive glory and honor and power, for you created all things, and by your will they were created and have their being. Worthy is the Lamb, who was slain, to receive power and wealth and wisdom and strength and honor and glory and praise! (Revelation 4:11; 5:12)

A Praise be to you, O Lord, God of our father Israel, from everlasting to everlasting. Yours, O Lord, is the greatness and the power and the glory and the majesty and the splendor, for everything in heaven and earth is yours. Yours, O Lord, is the kingdom; you are exalted as head over all. Wealth and honor come from you; you are the ruler of all things. In your hands are strength and power to exalt and give strength to all. Now, our God, we give you thanks, and praise your glorious name (1 Chronicles 29:10-13).

C Ascribe to the Lord, O mighty ones, ascribe to the Lord glory and strength. Ascribe to the Lord the glory due his name; worship the Lord in the splendor of his holiness (Psalm 29:1-2).

E I will extol the Lord at all times; his praise will
   always be on my lips. Glorify the Lord with me;
   let us exalt his name together (Psalm 34:1, 3).

APPLICATION - PRAYING FOR FREEDOM

13

When he taught us to pray in the Lord's prayer, "...deliver us from the evil one" (Matthew 9:13), Jesus made it clear that he knew we would be living in enemy territory. He knew that circumstances and forces of this world would victimize people and keep them from having the fullness in Christ that we covered in the last section. The New Testament teaches us that we have three opponents to contend with: the world, the flesh and the evil one.

John wrote, "Do not love the world or the things of the world. The love of the Father is not in them that love the world" (1 John 2:15). The world represents values, ideologies and structures that oppose God. For example, in John's gospel, Jesus is opposed by the religious systems that existed for themselves alone, and were void of the Spirit of God. The Pharisees and Sadducees, with whom Jesus occasionally exchanged words, characterized this influential structure. Today, many such systems exist that too often injure those who get caught up in their self-serving machinery. They need to be set free from the world.

The uncrucified human nature also opposes the rule of Jesus and caters to its own desires and pleasure. A good example of this is seen in Romans 7 where Paul reveals his own bitter struggle with the flesh. He describes it like a war between what he should do and what he wants to do. People will come for prayer who are addicted, depressed, and in conflict with the desires of their sinful natures—greed, immorality, dishonesty, hate, pride. They need to be set free from themselves.

Finally, some people are actually influenced or controlled by the evil one. They have an inside problem with an outside source. The Bible makes it clear that Satan and his army of fallen angels (demons) sometimes work very directly to oppress people, imprisoning them in behavior or thought patterns over which they have no control. Again, the ultimate goal is to keep them from enjoying life in Christ as it should be—victorious and full of joy. They need

IN AUTHORITATIVE PRAYER... WE ARE NOT SO MUCH SPEAKING *TO* GOD AS SPEAKING *FOR* GOD. —RICHARD FOSTER

to be set free from the enemy.

Jesus is the freedom bearer who came to set the captives free.

> The Spirit of the Lord is on me, because he has anointed me to preach good news to the poor. He has sent me to proclaim freedom for the prisoners and recovery of sight for the blind, to release the oppressed, to proclaim the year of the Lord's favor (Luke 4:18-19).

What he did then, he can do now. He sets us free from the world because he becomes our source for everything. And in his shed blood on the cross, he gave us power over sin, thereby defeating the enemy once and for all. As Paul declares, "And having disarmed the powers and authorities, he made a public spectacle of them, triumphing over them by the cross" (Colossians 2:15).

In the name of Jesus, you have the authority to break the cycle of oppression in someone's life. You can bring them to the Father and reinforce the work of Calvary on their behalf to set them free.

PRAYING GRACE FOR FREEDOM

G - God's Nature

As a prayer usher, when you encounter someone who is wrestling with one of these forces, it is always appropriate to focus first and foremost on the nature and greatness of God in her behalf. He is our rock of salvation (Psalm 27:5; 28:1), our shield and defender (Psalm 5:12; 7:10), and he is the one who gives us rest from our enemies. The Bible is full of scriptures to help us claim victory.

- The Lord will grant that the enemies who rise up against you will be defeated before you (Deuteronomy 28:7).

- O Lord, how many are my foes! How many rise up against me! Many are saying of me, "God will not deliver him." But you are a shield around me, O Lord; you bestow glory on me and lift up my

FOR OUR STRUGGLE IS NOT AGAINST FLESH AND BLOOD, BUT AGAINST THE RULERS, AGAINST THE AUTHORITIES, AGAINST THE POWERS OF THIS DARK WORLD AND AGAINST THE SPIRITUAL FORCES OF EVIL IN THE HEAVENLY REALMS.
—EPHESIANS 6:12

▣ ILLUSTRATION

Following a time of altar ministry at our church, I had the privilege of praying with a young woman who entered the counseling room leaning on her cane. It was obvious that every step was extremely painful and she could barely walk. She had suffered for years and asked me to pray for her healing.

As I began to pray, the Lord spoke to me, "Tell her that I forgive her!" I wrestled with this, not wanting to hurt her. But in obedience I said, "Before I pray for your healing, the Lord wants you to know he forgives you." She burst into tears and cried for a long time with deep sobs.

After we prayed for her healing, she said, " I know God is going to heal me," and he did. Today, years later, she is vibrant and active, selling fitness equipment. She says, "Forgiveness set me free and brought healing to my body."
—Vivian Summey, prayer usher at Hillcrest Church in Dallas, Texas

head. To the Lord I cry aloud, and he answers me from his holy hill. I lie down and sleep; I wake again, because the Lord sustains me. I will not fear the tens of thousands drawn up against me on every side. Arise, O Lord! Deliver me, O my God! Strike all my enemies on the jaw; break the teeth of the wicked. From the Lord comes deliverance. May your blessing be on your people (Psalm 3).

Pray: Arise O God and defeat all of _____'s enemies. Thank you for being a shield around her. As you promised Lord, bestow glory on her and lift her head. When she cries out to you, answer her and sustain her. She does not need to fear anything because you are her deliverer.

R – Righteousness of Jesus

As with any prayer, our prayer for freedom is heard in the name and finished work of Jesus Christ. We can take comfort in the fact that during his earthly ministry, he battled often with evil forces and was always victorious. When he took authority over them and commanded them, they had no choice but to submit to his lordship.

As I already mentioned, Jesus came to set the captives free and his death on the cross sealed the victory for all eternity. However, before he returned to heaven, he left specific instructions that we were to carry on his ministry to the oppressed (Mark 16:17) and he gave us the power of attorney to do this in his stead (Matthew 10:1). You have the ability, through Jesus, to pray against the forces of this world and be confident in victory. When you pray in Jesus' name for someone, you are reaffirming his ownership in her life and invoking his protection over her soul.

- The prayer of a righteous man is powerful and effective (James 5:16).

- Holy Father, protect them by the power of your name—the name you gave me—so that they may

be one as we are one. While I was with them, I protected them and kept them safe by that name you gave me (John 17:11-12).

- You performed miraculous signs and wonders in Egypt and have continued them to this day, both in Israel and among all mankind, and have gained the renown that is still yours (Jeremiah 32:20).

- You made a name for yourself, which remains to this day (Nehemiah 9:10).

- Therefore God exalted him to the highest place and gave him the name that is above every name, that at the name of Jesus every knee should bow, in heaven and on earth and under the earth, and every tongue confess that Jesus Christ is Lord, to the glory of God the Father (Philippians 2:10-11).

Pray: Thank you, Jesus, for setting the captives free, and for giving us the power to take authority over things that oppress us. We know our prayers for _____ today are effective because we bear your name and pray in and through you. You are exalted above everything, even _____ (insert what the person is struggling against) in _____'s life.

A - Ask

Truth has an innate spiritual power, and the Bible is truth. That is why we ask for personal liberty according to the scriptures.

Most bondage is based on a lie. For example, things such as fear, shame, confusion or helplessness that torment some people feed on thoughts or beliefs that are contrary to the mind of Christ for us as stated in the word. So we counter them with the truth about how God sees us and who we are in him. John stated it this way, "Then you will know the truth, and the truth will set you free" (John 8:32).

- And I will do whatever you ask in my name, so that the Son may bring glory to the Father. You may ask me for anything in my name, and I will

YOU ARE FREE IN CHRIST, BUT IF THE DEVIL CAN DECEIVE YOU INTO BELIEVING YOU'RE NOT, YOU WON'T EXPERIENCE THE FREEDOM WHICH IS YOUR IN-HERITANCE. I DON'T BELIEVE IN INSTANT MATURITY, BUT I DO BELIEVE IN INSTANT FREEDOM, AND I HAVE SEEN THOUSANDS OF PEOPLE SET FREE BY THE TRUTH. —NEIL T. ANDERSON

 NOTES

do it (John 14:13-14).

- You did not choose me, but I chose you and appointed you to go and bear fruit—fruit that will last. Then the Father will give you whatever you ask in my name (John 15:16).

- And surely I am with you always, to the very end of the age (Matthew 28:20).

Pray: Father, you have promised in your word that if we ask in Jesus' name, you will answer our prayer. I am asking today that you set _____ free from anything in her life that is keeping her from experiencing every good thing you have for her. By the blood of Jesus, break the hold of lies in her life, and fill her with your truth. Let _____ know that you are with her at all times, even when she is struggling.

C – *Confidence*

Our confidence in praying for freedom is entirely in God and his absolute authority in the heavens and earth. The power to overcome is not in our prayer, but in him.

- For it is we who...glory in Christ Jesus, and who put no confidence in the flesh... (Philippians 3:3).

Pray: Rejoice in the Lord now _____. Rejoice as an act of your will, not your feelings. The Lord is near! His peace is your guard in Jesus Christ and you can trust that he will go to work in your behalf. Your confidence lies in him, not in the flesh.

E – *Exaltation of Jesus*

We always want Jesus to be exalted as a result of our prayers on every occasion. The answer must call attention to him and never the one doing the praying. Be clothed in humility every time you pray for someone so that Jesus is the one that shines through.

- Do nothing out of selfish ambition or vain conceit, but in humility consider others better than

I WILL GIVE YOU THE KEYS OF THE KINGDOM OF HEAVEN; WHATEVER YOU BIND ON EARTH WILL BE BOUND IN HEAVEN, AND WHATEVER YOU LOOSE ON EARTH WILL BE LOOSED IN HEAVEN.
—MATTHEW 16:19

yourselves. You attitude should be the same as that of Christ Jesus: Who, being in very nature God, did not consider equality with God something to be grasped, but made himself nothing, taking the very nature of a servant, being made in human likeness (Philippians 2:3, 5-7).

- God exalted him to his own right hand as Prince and Savior that he might give repentance and forgiveness of sins to Israel (Acts 5:31).

- Yes, and I will continue to rejoice, for I know that through your prayers and the help given by the Spirit of Jesus Christ, what has happened to me will turn out for my deliverance. I eagerly expect and hope that I will in no way be ashamed, but will have sufficient courage so that now as always Christ will be exalted in my body, whether by life or by death (Philippians 1:18-20).

Pray: Lord, be exalted in _____'s life today through this prayer and forever. Be glorified in her mind, body and spirit as a testimony to your rule and reign above all things. You alone are worthy of our praise!

 NOTES

 PRACTICE SWINGS #1

Men: Frank is a Christian friend who confides in you that he has gotten hooked on internet pornography. He asks you to pray for him because he doesn't want to hurt his wife or family. Write out a prayer for him based on the GRACE card.

Women: Martha's daughter has just gone away to college and Martha says she is overcome with fear and anxiety for her child's safety. She is experiencing frequent panic attacks and is having trouble sleeping at night and functioning normally during the day. Although her daughter doesn't seem to be in any danger, Martha can't seem to control the fear. Write out a prayer for her based on the GRACE card.

G   The Lord is my light and my salvation—whom shall I fear? The Lord is the stronghold of my life—of whom shall I be afraid? When evil men advance against me to devour my flesh, when my enemies and my foes attack me, they will stumble and fall. Though an army besiege me, my heart will not fear; though war break out against me, even then will I be confident (Psalm 27:1-3).

R   Therefore, confess your sins to each other and pray for each other so that you may be healed. The prayer of a righteous man is powerful and effective (James 5:16).

So if the Son sets you free, you will be free indeed (John 8:36).

A   Then you will know the truth, and the truth will set you free (John 8:32).

He who did not spare his own Son, but gave him up for us all—how will he not also, along with him, graciously give us all things? No, in all these things we are more than conquerors through him who loved us (Romans 8:32, 37).

130

C If we confess our sins, he is faithful and just and will forgive us our sins and purify us from all unrighteousness. But if anybody does sin, we have one who speaks to the Father in our defense—Jesus Christ, the Righteous One. He is the atoning sacrifice for our sins, and not only for ours but also for the sins of the whole world (1 John 1:9; 2:1-2).

E Jesus Christ is the same yesterday and today and forever. Through Jesus, therefore, let us continually offer to God a sacrifice of praise—the fruit of lips that confess his name (Hebrews 13:8, 15).

NOTES

PRACTICE SWINGS #2

Bill and Nancy are committed Christians with a healthy marriage and family. He is a strong African American community leader in a town plagued with racial conflicts. Lately they say they have felt under attack.

Bill has been wrongly accused of some illegal dealings at work and his job is in jeopardy. Nancy's mother has recently been diagnosed with cancer. They are being sued by a group of irate neighbors for having a "house of prayer" sign in their yard. And their son just got kicked off the school football team for fighting, despite the fact that he is an honor student and says he was defending himself against serious racial threats. Write out a prayer for this family using the GRACE card.

APPLICATION - GRACE PRAYED

14

THE "WHATSOEVERS"

"And we know that he hears us, *whatsoever* we ask, we know that we have the petitions that we desire of Him" (1 John 5:15, KJV, italics mine).

In this final unit, we have looked at how to pray GRACE over four general prayer request topics: salvation, healing, fullness and freedom. Hopefully, through the teaching in the book and the practice exercises, you are getting more comfortable with the GRACE outline and using it with confidence.

Obviously it is impossible, either in the scope of this book or in your small group training, to prepare you for every manner of prayer request you will encounter as a prayer usher. That's what makes praying for people and watching God work in their individual lives such an amazing journey. But inevitably, the proverbial "What if" will come up. Consider these requests:

"I've just been laid off and I need to find another job."

"We're trying to buy a house, but we don't have the money for a down payment."

"My daughter is dating a young man that I think is a bad influence on her."

"I'm being sued by a former client for something I didn't do."

" My dog ran away and I want him to come home."

"Our son really wants to make the basketball team."

"I have a big presentation tomorrow. If it goes well, it could mean a promotion."

None of these people needs to be saved, healed or set free from anything, and they aren't really seeking to know God in a deeper or more profound way. What they want is for God to meet a felt need in their lives, a human desire that arises in the day to day business of living. Although these requests may not seem very

spiritual or even important in the scheme of the universe, they nevertheless matter to God simply because they matter to his children. He has promised to hear us when we pray, no matter *whatsoever* we ask of him, and these are the "whatsoevers."

One of the main purposes of this workbook was to teach you a model of personal prayer—praying GRACE—that is simple enough to remember and apply, yet flexible enough to be used for virtually any prayer request. And though I can't walk you through praying for the outcome of a local election, the weather for Saturday's big event, and a resolution to the conflict with in-laws, I can tell you that grace is sufficient to cover them all. You can pray God's nature in the righteousness of Jesus over any problem or concern, and then ask that Jesus be lifted up and exalted in the end result. In fact, consider how the following familiar prayer follows the GRACE outline:

> Our Father in heaven, hallowed be your name, your kingdom come, your will be done on earth as it is in heaven. Give us today _____. Forgive us our debts, as we also have forgiven our debtors. And lead us not into temptation, but deliver us from the evil one, for yours is the kingdom and the power and the glory forever. Amen (Matthew 6:9-13).

It is by grace that we have been saved, so that by grace we can ask God to help us face the challenges of this life.

WATER IN THE DESERT

Having lived most of my life in south Texas not far from the moist Gulf of Mexico breezes, I love the desert of Arizona. The arid climate that some find dry and dusty to me has a unique beauty all its own.

Several years ago I was in Phoenix doing a conference on the edge of the city. As I sometimes do before I teach, I was driving randomly throughout the surrounding area just to see where I was and get a feel for the community. When I got on an open road, I

ILLUSTRATION

As a young, very inexperienced preacher, I was praying at the altar one Sunday morning for a man in my church. He was kneeling in front of me and I had my hand on his head as a point of contact. I prayed so fervently that I failed to notice that in my vigor, I was "readjusting" the toupee on his head. By the time I finished praying, his hairpiece had migrated noticeably toward his left ear. I didn't know whether to discreetly stuff his hair into my pocket until a later, more private moment, or pray some more and try to move it back!

—Terry Teykl

could see the horizon in every direction because there was absolutely nothing blocking the view. The land was perfectly flat and there were no buildings to speak of except for the small wood frame houses of the neighborhoods. I drove around for several minutes, laughing to myself as I have many times before at the sight of yards covered with rocks instead of grass. Vegetation was non-existent. (Since yard work is always a major weekend activity in the lush, densely forested neighborhoods where I live, I always wonder what people who live in Arizona do with their Saturdays.)

Then suddenly, I turned a corner and encountered the most spectacular canvas of vivid color I have ever seen anywhere in America. As far as I could see, roses of every imaginable hue stretched out in long rows—crimson, chartreuse, dusty pink, candy apple red, lemon yellow, sunset orange, snowy white. I got out of the car. The smell was intoxicating.

Upon inquiring, I learned that it was a high volume rose farm where the plants were bred and raised, and then shipped all over the country. The hot, dry climate, so harsh and unforgiving to most green living things, when properly irrigated, is actually perfect for growing roses. What a difference water can make in the desert!

Where grace flows, spiritual lives will grow and flourish as well, even in hostile territory. God is the source of all good things, and his grace and love abound to us in infinite measure. By grace he forgives us, saves us, heals us and accepts us. And by grace he disciplines us, molds us and trains us to be his messengers of love to others. It is no wonder that one of our favorite hymns declares, "Amazing grace, how sweet the sound!"

> *Where grace flows, spiritual lives will grow and flourish as well, even in hostile territory.*

Prayer is the channel of grace. Like the giant aquaducts that bring water down from the mountain lakes to the middle of the

NOTES

desert, prayer brings forth the grace of heaven in a rushing current to thirsty souls. When we do personal ministry, whether in a church building or a hospital waiting room, we become conduits of God's unmerited favor. Grace prayed makes the difference.

ACTION AT THE ALTAR

Lives are being watered all over the country through churches and ministries that are praying grace. One of the best examples I know is a church here in Texas that I have known of and ministered in as a guest preacher many times, Hillcrest Church in Dallas.

One visit to the 17-year old, 5,000 member congregation is all it takes to see personal ministry in action. Senior pastor Dr. Morris Sheats believes strongly in the importance of altar ministry and he has made it a vital part of the church from its birth. Before the church even had a building, a trailer sat on the property as a place of prayer, and as the church has grown, it has always dedicated significant portions of its budget, building space and staff to prayer ministries. Dr. Walter Fletcher, the current full-time prayer minister, has been on staff with the church for 11 years and says that the prayer which takes place at the altars during worship services is a big reason many visitors find the church and make it their home. The ministry time is given equal, if not more, time and focus than the music or sermon.

Hillcrest actually has two distinct ministry times, each with its own purpose, time and trained volunteers. The first begins two or three songs into the worship time and lasts for the duration of worship, usually 15-20 minutes. Over 50 lay leaders, including many of the cell group leaders in the church, are trained for this ministry time which is aimed primarily at various kinds of healing. Dr. Sheats knows that often people arrive at church hurting, grieving, or carrying emotional baggage, and they need immediate attention. By praying for them and ministering to their pain, the prayer ushers help them prepare to receive the message.

 NOTES

The second ministry time takes place after the message is preached, and it is an opportunity for people to respond to what they have heard. More than 100 workers are trained for this personal ministry and many people make quality decisions for Christ during this second altar call.

Dr. Fletcher says that communicating to the prayer ushers the vision of altar ministry and giving them solid training are the keys to maintaining high standards and integrity. In fact, Dr. Fletcher and his team are doing such a good job of equipping their prayer rail ministers that other churches in the city are sending their own lay leaders to Hillcrest's annual three-day training session that includes workshops, guest speakers and hands-on practice.

Other churches as well are doing a first-rate job of personal prayer ministry. From Woodcrest United Methodist in East Texas, where they call their altar area the "grace station," to the Community of Joy Lutheran Church in Phoenix, Arizona, led by pastor Walt Kallestad. Community of Joy has found a way to remain committed to personal ministry despite the time pressure of their multiple services. People who want prayer following a service either meet a prayer usher at the front and are escorted to another room, or they are invited to the chapel where workers are waiting. Either way, prayer is given consistent support in a way that prevents the ministry encounters from being hampered by time constraints.

The entire movement of churches known as the Vineyard, started by John Wimber, practices altar ministry as a regular part of their worship time. In the one thousand Vineyard churches in this country and abroad, the ministry time comes at the end of the services. The Vineyard even has its own training manual that was developed to equip their altar workers, all of whom receive at least four to five hours of training for the ministry. Currently, an average of one new Vineyard congregation is started each week.

I spoke to the Atlanta Vineyard Church and learned that they allocate 15-30 minutes following the message for prayer, and generally see 20-30 people respond. They also hold a special worship and prayer service called "Unveiled" every other Friday night where more intense prayer can happen for longer periods of time.

Leaders of the Vineyard movement believe that their growth and vitality can be largely attributed to the worship and healing that people experience every Sunday.

Another dynamic church that is doing personal ministry is the Lakewood Church near downtown Houston. Started by John Osteen 55 years ago, Lakewood has become an icon in Houston, largely due to its reputation as a church that prays for people to be healed. In fact, Lakewood's influence is global, thanks to a national and international television ministry, and many people travel across the country and around the globe just to come kneel at the altars and receive prayer.

And while some may be skeptical about the thousands of testimonies of how God has answered those prayers, it's hard to argue with a Sunday morning attendance of 24,000. And even harder if you understand that the church sits buried in the industrial, east side of the city, far removed from anything new, suburbian or upper class.

> *Even with a Sunday morning attendance of 24,000, Joel Osteen has never questioned his father's philosophy of praying and ministering personally to individuals.*

Yet even though they run three services each weekend averaging 8,000 each, young Joel Osteen, who took over leadership of the congregation several years ago upon the death of his father, has never questioned his father's philosophy of praying and ministering personally to individuals. If anything, he has stepped up the intensity.

Every service at Lakewood starts with worship, followed by a time of prayer when the altars are open. Hundreds of trained altar workers surround the platform area and pray with the many

 NOTES

that come forward. The Osteen family often prays with special visitors who have travelled long distances in the hopes of receiving healing. Another invitation is offered after the message for any who would like to receive Christ, and they too are prayed for personally in a separate room designated for follow-up ministry.

While I have known about Lakewood's personal ministry for many years, I gained an even deeper respect for the church during the devastating floods last summer caused by tropical storm Allison. I saw that personal ministry is not just something they do on Sunday morning to draw in a crowd; it is truly at the very heart and soul of the leadership and the body.

On the east side of Houston, which was hit the hardest with flood waters that literally covered homes and swept away people's lives, Lakewood became an island not just of spiritual help, but love in action. Within days, their entire facility was transformed into a relief center for the victims. For weeks, all normal church business was put on hold and services were cancelled because the 8,000 seat auditorium had become a shelter for familes who had no place to go. With help from the Red Cross and thousands of people who lined up daily to bring donations of food, clothing and water, not withholding any of their own resources, the church housed and fed hundreds of mothers, fathers and children who had lost everything. They ministered in word and deed to anyone and everyone who came through their doors. No one was turned away.

> *Prayer rolled up its sleeves, put on work clothes, and became the tangible compassion and love of Jesus.*

I know it is true, as I mentioned before, that when a congregation learns to pray and minister to each other, the spirit of personal prayer ministry becomes a part of who they are as individuals, and they take that with them out into the community where it shines in the darkness. Lakewood's response during that time of crisis was a beautiful example. Prayer rolled up its sleeves, put on work clothes,

and became the tangible compassion and love of Jesus.

I don't know how many of those people who slept in the sanctuary made professions of faith in Jesus Christ, nor how many of them might have become regular Lakewood church members as a result of their experience. But I do know that everyone who passed through the building during that time *saw* the gospel. Prayer doesn't just affect those we pray for; it changes us as well.

Looking to the future, Lakewood Church has just recently signed a ten-year lease on Houston's former basketball arena known as the Compaq Center. Seating capacity—18,000.

Another example of personal prayer making a big difference outside the church is through the ministry known as Walk to Emmaus. Started by the Catholics and later adopted, adapted and renamed by the Methodists, the Walk to Emmaus movement has grown to serve 50,000 to 60,000 people each year. Its name is derived from the passage in Luke 24:13-35 when the resurrected Lord appeared and walked with two of the disciples on the road to Emmaus. The idea is that the "pilgrims," as participants are called, will recognize Jesus in a new way just as the two disciples did.

Currently there are 280 Walk to Emmaus communities in the United States and at least 70 more abroad. Each community is a geographically connected group of individuals who have been on a Walk in the past and now serve as intercessors and volunteers for Emmaus weekends in their area. The level of involvement these communities have in the ministry on an ongoing basis is a good indicator of just how meaningful the experience is.

Much of the Emmaus philosophy and success is born out of soaking, intensive personal prayer for individuals. Pilgrims must be invited or sponsored to go on a Walk, and the potential candidates and the entire invitation process are bathed in prayer. Once participants are confirmed, they leave for a 72 hour weekend that begins on Thursday evening and ends on Sunday evening.

Throughout the Walk to Emmaus, pilgrims are prayed for

GRACE IS CHRISTIANITY'S BEST GIFT TO THE WORLD, A SPIRITUAL NOVA IN OUR MIDST EXERTING A FORCE STRONGER THAN VENGEANCE, STRONGER THAN RACISM, STRONGER THAN HATE. —PHILIP YANCEY

 NOTES

off-site by one of the nearby communities, as well as on site in a round-the-clock vigil in which volunteer intercessors pray for each one by name. They experience heavy doses of corporate prayer in the meetings, small group prayer among themselves, and prayer combined with worship and communion.

My own brother-in-law, who had been a churchgoer for years, accepted Christ for the first time on a Walk to Emmaus in response to the very personal prayer and ministry lavished on each individual that comes. Although salvation is not a major theme, most participants say they discover a profound new intimacy with God in the prayer-drenched atmosphere. How much more might people get out of church services if we did a better job of soaking them in prayer before, during and after the fact?

I'd like to leave you with one last example of grace being prayed on the mission front, because in many ways, we in America have no concept of how great an impact prayer is having in other countries. Years ago, a man named Danny Ost received a vision of millions of people perishing in Mexico without knowing Jesus. The image in his mind so disturbed him that, though he could not articulate the details of the vision, it became a focusing point of his missionary career. He devoted the latter part of his life to saving lost souls in Mexico, and his passion led to the formation of the largest residential Bible School in the country as well as several Faith, Hope and Love Centers. These centers held services every hour between 9:00 in the morning and 10:00 in the evening, every day, six days a week, all year long. Simultaneously, they taught special Bible and practical living classes.

What struck me as I read about these centers in the Dedication of the book *Loving Your City into the Kingdom* by Ted Haggard and Jack Hayford, was that following every one-hour service, altar workers prayed with those who repsonded to the altar calls, essentially leading people to Christ all day long. Ted writes:

> Because the services were scheduled so tightly,
> the altar-call music for one service became the

INTERCESSION IS NOT A SUBSTITUTION FOR SIN. BUT INTERCESSION SO IDENTIFIES THE INTERCESSOR WITH THE SUFFERER THAT IT GIVES HIM A PREVAILING PLACE WITH GOD. HE MOVES GOD. HE EVEN CAUSES HIM TO CHANGE HIS MIND.
—NORMAN GRUBB

music for the following service. The flow of people coming and going was constant. The result was a cycle of worshipping, praying, coming to Christ and being discipled—all because of a passion for souls.

GETTING HOLD OF PRAYER

When I think about things like that happening in Mexico, Korea, Uganda, South America and other regions where so many are starving for the gospel, I have to look at our American churches and wonder if we are not missing some vital understanding of the urgency of ministering per-

> *I have to wonder if we are not missing some vital understanding of the urgency of ministering personally to people.*

sonally to people instead of shuffling them in and out of our buildings like spectators at an opera. I have to wonder, as I did at the beginning of this book, what Jesus would think if he were to visit one of our churches today where he might sing songs, listen to a sermon and pass the plate, and then file out, without ever having any personal interaction with people except for polite pleasantries.

In my very first pastorate I was privileged to have three brothers, George, Lester and Edwin. Though all were precious country folk who loved the Lord with everything they had, George was the one who left a lasting impression on both me and that rural church. In fact, George, who lived across the street from the church, came so often that his heavy work boots wore the varnish off the floor beneath his front row seat.

George owned the sawmill in town and he was a big, hard-working man. The noise of the mill had taken its toll on his hearing though, so I always tried to preach loud so George could hear. I knew how much he had caught of my sermon by what he said to me on the way out the door.

Back in those days, when I served communion, I walked up and down the altar rails where people knelt with two brass plates,

 NOTES

one filled with small, flat wafers, and the other with juice-filled communion cups. George's hands were so big and calloused that I always had to give him just a little extra time to carefully pick up the elements. I remember one day watching his fingers scratch around the bottom of that shiny brass dish, trying so hard to get a hold of one of the delicate wafers. And I thought to myself, "How hard it is for all of us to really grasp what a sacrament is."

When it comes to communicating with God and his desire to interact with us, I feel like George, scratching around in the bottom of the dish, trying so hard to get a hold of the mystery. I don't understand it all, but I know I want to partake of everything that can happen in the divine encounter called prayer.

WORKS CITED

Neil T. Anderson. *The Bondage Breaker*. Eugene, OR: Harvest House Publishers, 1993, p. 12.

George Barna. *Evangelism that Works*. Ventura, CA: Regal Books, 1995, p. 53.

Roxanne Brant. *Ministering to the Lord*. Naples, FL: Outreach for Christ, Inc., 1973, p. 18.

Reginald Cherry, M.D. *Healing Prayer*. Nashville, TN: Thomas Nelson, 1999, p. 69-71.

Judson Cornwall. *Praying the Scriptures*. Lake Mary, FL: Creation House, 1990, back cover.

Maxie Dunham. *Unless We Pray*. Nashville, TN: The Upper Room, 1989, p. 17.

Richard Foster. *Prayer: Finding the Heart's True Home*. New York, NY: HarperCollins Publishers, 1992, p. 229.

Francis Frangipane. *Holiness, Truth and the Presence of God*. Cedar Rapids, IA: Arrow Publications, 1986, p. 24, 27.

Jonathan Graf. *The Power of Personl Prayer*. Colorado Springs, CO: Navpress, 2002, p. 179.

Norman Grubb. *Rees Howells Intercessor*. Fort Washington, PA: Christian Literature Crusade, 1952, p. 84.

Ted Haggard and Jack Hayford. *Loving Your City into the Kingdom*. Ventura, CA: Regal Books, 1997, p. 3.

Dudley Hall. *Incense and Thunder*. Sisters, OR: Multnomah Publishers, 1999, p. 200-201.

Jack Hayford. *A Man's Walk with God*. Nashville, TN: Thomas Nelson, 1993, p. 10-11.

Evan B. Howard. *Praying the Scriptures*. Downers Grove, IL: InterVarsity Press, 1999.

David Jeremiah. *Prayer the Great Adventure*. Sisters, OR: Multnomah Publishers, 1997, p. 58.

Peter Lord. *Hearing God*. Grand Rapids, MI: Baker Book House, 1988, p. 211.

Fawn Parish. *Honor*. Ventura, CA: Renew, 1999, p. 68, 77.

Dr. Margaret Poloma. "The Spirit and the Bride: The Toronto Blessing and Church Structure." *Evangelical Studies Bulletin*. Wheaton, IL: Wheaton College, Vol. 13, No. 4, Winter, 1996.

Trisha Rhodes. *The Soul at Rest*. Minneapolis, MN: Bethany House, 1996, p. 16.

Oral Roberts. *Seed-Faith Commentary on the Holy Bible*. Tulsa, OK: Pinoak Publications, 1975, p. 133-134.

Agnes Sanford. *Behold Your God*. St. Paul, MN: Macalester Park Publishing Company, 1958, p. 28.

Ed Silvoso. *Prayer Evangelism*. Ventura, CA: Regal Books, 2000, p. 151.

Ed Silvoso. *That None Should Perish*. Ventura, CA: Regal Books, 1994, p. 80.

Jack Taylor. *Prayer: Life's Limitless Reach*. Nashville, TN: Broadman Press, 1977, p. 22.

Terry Teykl. *Blueprint for the House of Prayer*. Muncie, IN: Prayer Point Press, 1997, p. 60.

Terry Teykl. *Box 3:16 Prayer Evangelism for the Marketplace*. Muncie, IN: Prayer Point Press, 2001.

Terry Teykl. *How to Pray After You've Kicked the Dog*. Muncie, IN: Prayer Point Press, 1999, p. 128.

Terry Teykl. *Outside the Camp*. Muncie, IN: Prayer Point Press, 2001, p. 12.

Elmer Towns and Neil T. Anderson. *Rivers of Revival*. Ventura, CA: Regal Books, 1997, p. 198-200.

B. J. Willhite. *Why Pray?* Altamonte Springs, FL: Creation House, 1988, p. 91.

Philip Yancey. *What's So Amazing About Grace?* Grand Rapids, MI: Zondervan Publishing House, 1997, p. 29, 30, 69.